Rebound

To Kia Always The Best

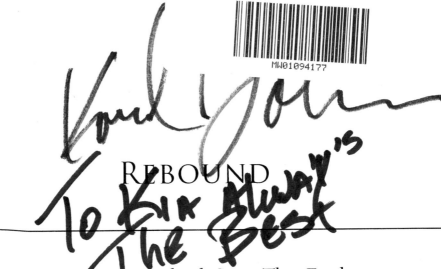

An Inspiring Comeback Story That Explores

The Mystery Of The Human Spirit

To Kia – Give others hope!

Karl Johnson and
Samantha Bauer

ISBN: 1493683799
ISBN 13: 9781493683796
Library of Congress Control Number: 2013921180
CreateSpace Independent Publishing Platform
North Charleston, South Carolina

DEDICATION

To MY BIG brother and best friend—Dennis Wayne Johnson. I miss you.

Dennis (left) and Karl Johnson. San Pedro, California. Circa 1981.

Foreword by Karl Johnson

My name is Karl Johnson, and I have a story to tell. It is a story of missed shots and a lot of losing. I hope that my story will inspire young people to make the right choices. While I have many regrets, I am filled with gratitude for the life I have today.

Playing basketball for Los Angeles Harbor College, I never knew I would end up homeless more than thirty years later in Fresno. I am one of sixteen children and had a brother who was a five-time NBA All-Star and Hall of Famer. I took the wrong path—he did not. I had a future. But I made the wrong choices, leading me down a path that landed me in state prison for nearly eleven years.

I was told it would be difficult to find work once I was released—no one wanted to hire someone with a criminal record. I tried for eighty days to find a job, and then decided it was time to leave LA behind. In January 2011, I jumped on a bus and headed north. I was on a two-hour layover in Fresno and decided instead this was the place for a fresh start. I had $400 in my pocket, and this town needed a good shoeshine.

I shined shoes downtown and on a good day would make thirty dollars—not enough to keep me off the streets, where I lived until being placed in an apartment in November 2011, thanks to Fresno First Steps Home program.

There's a lot of good people in this town. Without them and God, I wouldn't be here on my rebound. It's never too late to be on the rebound of your life. The final buzzer is far from sounding on my comeback. I know that there are many slam dunks ahead.

It is with the grace of God that I finally "got it." Mama had faith that I would someday "get it," and I did. For that I am grateful.

This is a story about my rebound. I have a second chance, and I'm running with it.

Message from Co-Author Samantha Bauer

I met Karl Johnson while doing a writing project for *Fresno First Steps Home*.

I was there to capture his story. He handed me two ratty notebooks to prove that he had been writing. Eleven years of writing in state prison, yielding pages filled with accounts of his brother's ascent into NBA greatness against the backdrop of his own life of drugs, violence, and crime. I held the notebooks and a photo of him and Dennis Johnson in my hands, moved by an emotion that I couldn't quite grasp in that moment.

I wanted to know more, but I was there to do a job. My gut told me there was so much more to his story than what I captured that day.

I would not discover the richness of his story until much later. Fate would interfere once more. Nearly a year after our first encounter, I saw him shining shoes downtown. We exchanged phone numbers and agreed to meet that Saturday.

Our journey writing together began when I bought him a cup of coffee. I sat and listened to him for hours. Motivated to help him write his story, I joined Karl on his journey. My inspiration for devoting my time to give wings to his voice is about exploring the mystery of the human spirit. I needed to know why and how Karl found himself on a successful rebound.

I have learned a lot about regrets and the power of second chances. I have cried and laughed, learning about his pain and writing his story. I am thankful for Karl's family who taught him to work hard and never give up. I am grateful for the opportunity to be a part of Karl's rebound.

I will miss seeing "Coffee with Karl" on my calendar every Wednesday at 9 a.m., but our journey continues to live in our blog. One of my blog posts sums up our experience well:

> *April, 2013*
> *Gratitude in the listening*
> *He said "thanks" today. Thanks for listening to him. It has been very therapeutic, he says. I do a lot of listening because there is magic in his voice, and I want to capture his authenticity. Hours of his voice on tape, chronicling stories that prompt sadness, laughter, and insight. His story is powerful – I believe in the message that it's never too late to right the path you're on. I am grateful for our journey together. I am grateful for the family that raised him. I am grateful for his will to live the life he is meant to live.*
> *He is grateful for me listening. I am grateful for his voice.*
> *Gratitude – it's a two-way street, for sure.*

Introduction by Renee Johnson James

I am honored to have a chance to write an introduction for this amazing book about two young men who grew up together, but grew so far apart as their lives went in different directions. I know because I grew up with them both and saw how their own choices led them down different paths. The individual journeys that both Karl and Dennis traveled are incredible and amazing in their own right. I know readers will enjoy *Rebound* because anyone who knows Karl, knows that you are in for quite a ride!

Thank you, Karl, for allowing me, your sister, to be a part of your journey. I know that Daddy and Mama are so proud.

Renee Johnson James

ACKNOWLEDGMENTS

WE OWE A lot of people our sincere gratitude for making this book possible. Thank you to all my brothers and sisters for their continued love and support. Thank you to Donna for taking care of my brother and being a good wife to him. To all the good people in Fresno—thank you to my friend, Victor Salazar, who was my lucky charm. Thank you to my good friend, Tim Cox, for being there for me. Thank you to the Downtown Club for finally giving me a job. Thank you to Charles Doerksen for giving Samantha Bauer and me a quiet place to write *Rebound*. Thank you to Rick and Jeff Roush for providing a space for Anytime Shoe Shine. Thank you to the Fresno Housing Authority for the good work you do for so many people—special thanks to Preston Prince, Angie Nguyen, and Tiffany Cantu. Thank you to Fresno Mayor Ashley Swearengin for leading with your heart. Thank you to the United Way for giving me a chance to have a purpose and an opportunity to positively impact others. Thank you to Kristine Walter and Wheelhouse Strategies for the outstanding support and encouragement. A special thank you to Kenny Green for always being there when others were not. Finally, thank you to Paul, Maddy, and Max for your support and "lending" your wife and mom to help *Rebound* come alive.

PROLOGUE

Lil' Red is dead.

This is all I can think as I walk the track out in the prison yard.

My boys are huddled around me, forming a circle to shield me from exposing my pain to other inmates. There is no crying in prison. You don't show weakness.

They can't shield me from this pain. Tears are running down my face, and I think I am sobbing. I keep walking until I can't go anymore. I fall to my knees.

My hero is dead.

He taught me about hard work. About being the best at whatever you do. I'm one of the best inmates there is and known for my no-nonsense ways. I'm earning points to shave off time from my sentence. I'm in my seventh year of serving a twenty-two-year sentence for selling and transporting cocaine—I was one of the best runners of cocaine in LA. But no court can match the lifetime sentence I am serving for *using* the cocaine.

I saw his face on the TV this morning, but I couldn't hear what the reporter was saying. It is not unusual to see his face on TV.

Maybe he has finally been voted into the Basketball Hall of Fame.

The guard called for me.

Something is terribly wrong.

The guard took me to a room and handed the phone to me. The voice on the other end said he'd had a heart attack while coaching the Austin Toros—he'd collapsed on the court and died today.

I feel a hand on my arm. One of my boys is trying to help me up off the dirt.

"Come on, Karl—it will be OK."

No it won't. We have unfinished business.

"We will cross that bridge when we get there."

These words pound in my head—they are the last words he said to me on the phone. We will never cross that bridge together.

My brother is dead.

Chapter One

The invention of basketball was not an accident.
It was developed to meet a need.
—James Naismith

It's 1965, and the four of us boys are lying in our beds in our house in Wilmington, a small community in the Los Angeles Harbor area. I share a bunk with Dennis, but we don't call him Dennis or DJ, which he will eventually become known as on the NBA court. We call him Lil' Red because of his red hair and freckles. Just like our mother with the red hair and freckles. Some of us got the freckles and some of us got the dark skin. I got the dark skin.

Gary—who we call "Big Red"—and David share the other bunk. We are making plans for when we make it in professional basketball. We talk about what we would do for each other. We all want to play for the Lakers, and when one of us makes it big, we agree that our little group will be taken care of—it's our pact.

Lots of people dream about being doctors and lawyers. We just want to entertain and play ball.

We are raised in a large family—I am number nine in what eventually will be a lineup of sixteen children. Because there are so many of us, we are raised in "groups"—my group includes my older brothers, Gary, Dennis, David, and my younger sister, Renee. Each group has one girl—kind of strange how that worked out. Renee and I are closest in age, and Mama relies on Renee a lot for help with the house and the kids. The strong bond between Mama and Renee will contribute to jealousy later on, but Renee is solid when it comes to helping out. She's the go-to for Mama—and for me.

I'm eight years old, and all I can think about is basketball. I pull my blanket up over me and stare at the ceiling. No fancy bedspreads. Just blankets Mama got at Pick-N-Save. She gets everything there. When Daddy cut our hair into the high-water fad and made our cutline too high, she bought us all ten-cent hats to wear to school, so no one would make fun of us. To everyone else, it looked like Daddy put a bowl over our heads. It was so embarrassing.

But I'm not thinking about that. I'm thinking about how I want to be Jerry West and Walt Frazier, as I fall asleep.

I wake to the smell of smoke.

"Hey, guys, wake up. I smell smoke," I say.

"Go back to sleep, knucklehead," David says.

"No, I'm serious."

"Shut up, Karl, go back to sleep!" Gary says.

Gary is always bossing me around.

I get up and go to the door. It's closed like it is every night. I open it, but I am met with a burst of heat. The smoke chokes me.

"Fire!"

Dennis, Gary, and David jump up, and we all go to the window to climb out. I run around the house to my parents' window and bang on the window.

The scene from the outside is scarier than inside. Smoke is piling out of the windows, and the flames are angrily taking over our three-bedroom house.

We are assembled in the backyard on the full-sized basketball court that Daddy built for us. He is a cement mason and used his craft to transform our backyard into a dream-producing cement court.

Mama is crying. Her red hair is almost all gone—singed by the fire as she ran through the house gathering kids. Daddy is counting heads. At this time, there are nine of us living in the house and we are one head short—my little sister, Janett, is still in the house.

This is happening so fast. We are yelling and running around. I see my older brothers, Charles and Tony, go back into the house to get her.

My legs feel like they are a hundred pounds each. I am frozen by panic, as I watch Tony and Charlie—who has no legs and no prostheses—climb back into that window to get my sister.

Charlie lost his legs when he was ten years old. I was just a brand-new baby when it happened. Charlie and his friends would jump on one of the boxcars along the Pacific Coast Highway and ride it into school. On May 1, 1957, he and his friends came home for lunch—that's what they did then. On their way back to school, Charlie's pants leg got caught in the wheels and several boxcars ran over his legs, crushing them below the knees. My brother, Tony, ran to get Mama, and a man who owned a business nearby pulled Charlie out, tying a rope around his legs to stop the bleeding. That man probably saved Charlie's life, but not his legs.

The railroad is big here in Wilmington—this is where the first railroad was built in Los Angeles in the 1860s. Wilmington was founded by a guy named Phineas Banning, who named it after his birthplace of Wilmington, Delaware. He is also known as the "father of the Port of Los Angeles."

I hear baby sister Janett screaming before I see Tony and Charlie come out around the other side of the house. Tony is carrying her and gives her to Mama. Mama grabs the baby and squeezes her so tight that I think Mama is going to hurt her. Both Tony and Charlie are gasping for air, but their heaving doesn't match Mama's sobbing and Janett screaming.

"Praise the Lord," Mama repeats, as we all huddle together in the midst of the flames eating up our house.

The house that Daddy bought with his veteran's loan has now burned to the ground. Daddy fought in the Korean War and earned the opportunity to buy a brand-new house for his family.

Someone had left the TV on and it caught fire. It was a big console TV positioned in front of the window. Once the curtains caught fire, the house was history. The TV that fed our dreams, as we watched magic on the NBA basketball court, burned down our house and everything in it.

Chapter Two

Everything happens for a reason. I'm used to it, I prepare for it. Like I say, at the end of the day, those in charge of their own destiny are going to do what's right for them and their family.

—Shaquille O'Neal

We move in with my grandparents on Upland Avenue, a tree-lined street in San Pedro. There are two houses on the property, and we stay in the two-bedroom house in the back. Mama works in social services, and she knows how to access the resources to get us clothing and basic household items that we lost in the fire.

Grand-mama and Jason live in the front house. My mama is their only child. They moved to California from Holly Springs, Mississippi, when Mama was just thirteen years old. It explains why Mama had sixteen children—she was probably lonely growing up. We don't call Jason "Grandpa"—we just call him Jason, which is not even his real name. His name is Rudolph. We will find out years later that Jason is not Mama's real dad.

Grand-mama has these two dogs that I don't like. Heidi is the big red dog, and then there's a Chihuahua named Junior. Grand-mama treats these dogs like they are children, letting them sit on the couch, and we have to sit on the floor. I can't stand these dogs, but that Chihuahua started a whole generation of Chihuahuas in the Johnson family.

I'll put up with these dogs for Grand-mama's fried chicken and potato salad. She makes the best potato salad with Miracle Whip, relish, eggs, and onions—there's no better potato salad out there.

I like it here, and it's not just because of the food. The neighborhood is real nice with lots of hills. Dennis, Gary, and I get a bunch of cardboard from the factories and flatten them out to make them into sleds. We are sliding down the hills for fun on that cardboard.

I take a running start and jump on the cardboard. I get to going fast and can't stop, ending up on Channel Avenue. We have no business on Channel Avenue with all of the cars. It's so dangerous, and I love it.

I get down the hill almost in the middle of that busy street and here comes the big, ugly red truck that Jason drives.

"Ya'll get outta that street now!"

Jason is a junkman hauling junk during the day and works at a liquor store at night. You can see him coming around that corner because he has the biggest, ugliest red truck loaded down with all this junk.

I swear, years later I thought that *Sanford and Son* TV show was modeled on Jason. Red Foxx had the same big old truck, collecting junk just like Jason.

Jason is retired from the navy and just a hard worker. He's an excellent baseball player, too. He played for the old Negro league and plays in Wilmington for the semi-professional club, where we shag balls for twenty-five cents a ball. He hits lots of foul balls, and we think that he does it on purpose to take care of us.

Jason wants Dennis and me to play baseball. This doesn't make Daddy happy because Daddy wants us to play basketball. They clash all the time, but I never hear Jason say anything bad about Daddy, except to warn us about the drink.

"Don't be no drinker like your daddy," he says.

You can't get past Jason. He's in charge here. Dennis, David, and I are walking to school one morning, and we pass Jason, sitting on the front porch. He sits on that great big old front porch a lot, sipping his wine and smoking his cigar.

But not this morning. Today, he's got a baseball bat in his hands just waiting for us to come out of the back house. He's left-handed and standing on that front porch ready to swing.

"You boys come up here, now. I'm gonna show you how to swing this bat."

He's always trying to teach us something. I tell him maybe later because we have to get to school. We give him the respect that he demands because he is good to us.

He even lets us raid his lunchbox. It's a good day when he has those little sausages in there. There's always so much food in there that I think he must have gone by the store after work to refill it.

Every night, Jason invites us to the kitchen table and pours Dennis, Gary, David, and me a cup of black coffee placed on a saucer. It's kind of fancy, and we think this is cool—we are acting like adults. Daddy doesn't let us do adult things. We are not allowed to speak when adults are speaking. We have to stay out of the way of adults. When Daddy has grown-ups over, we have to be in the back room away from the adults.

So, the fact that we are sitting there at the kitchen table sipping coffee is a big deal.

Jason's teaching us about life, talking about the South. I don't think the South ever left him, and even though I'm only eight years old, I can see that he was hurt by the South. He tells us about Mississippi and all the bad stuff that happened there. He's telling stories about how we need to be careful hanging out with white people. I don't understand this.

Mama teaches us that people are people. The color of their skin doesn't mean anything. I'm just friends with everybody.

Even though I'm new at the elementary school around the corner, I make friends fast. That's the thing about sports. It just brings kids together, but later I will find out that it also creates fights.

I invite my new friend, Danny, to come over and play after school. We are walking by the front house, and there's Jason sitting in his chair on the porch.

"Karl, you come on over here, now," he yells out.

I run up the porch steps, and Danny follows.

"You just stay there, boy. I gotta talk to Karl," Jason says to Danny. He's polite, but firm.

"What you doing bringing him here?" He's whispering, but I can tell he's mad.

"He's my friend."

"What did I tell you now? He can't be here."

He doesn't say it, but I know why Danny can't be here. Danny is white.

I'm a little sad. I tell Danny that I got a bunch of chores to do, and I can't play today. Danny leaves.

"You just gotta be careful. This stuff can be turned into something that it's not," he says, as I walk to the little house in the back. My head hangs down a bit. I'm sad and confused.

Something what? Mama always tells me not to pick my friends by the color of their skin.

Jason knows what he's talking about when it comes to baseball. He just doesn't understand that this isn't Mississippi.

It takes less than a year to rebuild our house in Wilmington. It's time to go home. I know I will miss the nightly teachings by Jason, sipping coffee. But we are all happy to go to our own home.

They rebuilt our house exactly how it was before the fire. We are so happy to come back. But, we will only stay in that house a year before moving to Compton. When the time comes to move, I'm crying. I don't want to leave the house I grew up in.

I don't like moving.

But according to Mama, we are moving up.

"This is a good thing, Karl. You will see. It's a much better neighborhood and bigger house," she explains.

We move into a split-level home in Compton on Burris Avenue. We have a great big bedroom with two sets of bunk beds on each side of the room and two flat beds—there's ten of us sleeping in that room. The older boys get the flat beds—not me. I never get the good stuff.

Now I see why Compton is considered a nice place to live and a step up from Wilmington. Our house is right across the street from Emerson Elementary School, and in the back is Roosevelt Junior High School, where Dennis, Gary, David, and I play basketball. We stay out there all day just playing ball until Mama comes out of the house and yells for us to come in.

We play with the Davis family boys, who live down the street in the middle of the block—there are nine boys in their family. We are always either fighting them or playing ball with them. Even the Davis sisters get in on the action. Dennis always fights Charlotte—she's the oldest sibling, and there's a tension there that I won't understand until I hit puberty.

One day we are fighting, just hitting and pushing each other, and the next day we are all friends again. Alliances are big here in Compton. Even then, battle lines are beginning to be drawn.

Compton will bring us opportunity—the good and the bad. There's a reason we are here.

Chapter Three

I really don't like talking about money. All I can say is that the Good Lord must have wanted me to have it.
—Larry Bird

Shenanigans. Tomfoolery. Mischief. Call it what you will, but my brothers and I are always up to something. There is a lot of *something* going on for us young boys.

It's Saturday morning, and there are chores to do. We have chores to do every day before school and on weekends. We have to do dishes, take care of our baby sister, clean the bathroom, and take the garbage out. We can't leave the house until chores are done. My brothers don't want to do chores, so they make me do them.

Today, it's hot and we want to go to the pool, but I have to finish mowing the lawn before we can go.

Every Saturday, Mama gives us each a dollar. A dollar goes a long way in the 1960s. This covers our entrance to the pool for twenty-five cents and a hot dog for ten cents, but we are scheming about ways to make more money.

On our way to the pool, there is a bowling alley and restaurant with about twenty tables. We come up with a plan for lifting some of the tips.

"You and David go in there and start fightin' real good," Gary says.

Gary is in charge. He's good at giving orders. He will eventually become the first black elected dispatcher at the Port of Los Angeles, doling out the jobs. He sure knows how to tell us what to do.

It's time to act. It's time to fight.

So, David and I go into the restaurant, and we are over there fighting. Just fighting like crazy, but we are not even hitting each other. Just cussing and spitting at each other. We are bad. The waiters and some of the customers run over to break up the fight, while Gary and Dennis grab some of the tips off the tables. They run out the back, and David and I run out the entrance.

We come away with about fifteen dollars. But I get the short end of the stick. I always get the short end of the stick.

"Come on! I want my fair share."

"Knock it off, Karl—you don't need that many chili dogs," Gary says.

When we get to the pool, Gary and Dennis get all these sodas and food. I'm left with a chili dog.

We go back to that bowling alley a couple more times. The trick is to catch someone who doesn't know us.

I feel kind of bad because it is sort of like stealing.

Soon the gig is up—they all know us at the bowling alley, so we start shagging balls at the Dodgers farm team field down the street at Kelly Field. We shag balls, and we sit in the back of Kelly Field in our tree house that we built up with a bunch of wood we found in the neighborhood.

The tree house is our clubhouse, and this is our escape. It's also our meeting place to come up with a plan for making more money. We have some blankets up there to sit on, and it is also where we hide the boxes of Frosted Flakes and cans of fruit cocktail that we swipe from one of the boxcars sitting on the train tracks. It's amazing to me how easy it is to jump on those boxcars and grab the goods. Daddy would give us a whipping if he knew we were even getting close to the train tracks, let alone jumping on the boxcars. I think Daddy blames himself for what happened to Charlie, but it's not Daddy's fault that the train car ruined Charlie's legs.

Our tree house overlooks the backyard of a guy named Conrad. I'm afraid that big old Conrad—I swear, he weighs like three hundred pounds—is going to see our loot and turn us in, so I come up with the idea to give him a few boxes of Frosted Flakes to keep him quiet. We buy milk with the money we get from collecting bottles in the neighborhood, and we eat Frosted Flakes in bowls we borrow from Mama's kitchen.

We are like little business dudes, eating our Frosted Flakes and planning for our next big scheme to make money. And we have dreams of playing professional basketball.

Chapter Four

Young people need models, not critics
—John Wooden

We are all piled in Mama's blue Chevy Impala on our way to the Forum to see the LA Lakers play against the Boston Celtics. Gary gets the front seat. I guess that's what happens when you are in charge.

Sports are big in our house, and Daddy makes sure we have enough money for tickets to see at least one sporting event a month. He works all the time, so Mama takes us to see the Dodgers and the Lakers play.

I'm in the backseat with David and Dennis, and I'm so excited to see my favorite player, Happy Hairston.

"Happy's gonna kill it today," I say from the backseat.

"Yeah, I can't wait to see them beat the Celtics," Dennis says.

We don't like the Boston Celtics. None of us in that car will understand the irony of this until we are cheering for DJ on the Celtics' court years later.

Happy wears number 52, and I love the way he plays the game. He stands at six-feet, seven inches, but in my mind, he's ten feet tall.

He's a tough guy, and I want to be him.

We stop off at the convenience store to get some candy. Mama already fed us before we left, but she gives us each a dollar to buy some candy to eat at the game. I grab my favorite, Mr. Goodbar, and Dennis is grabbing a load of Kits—they are square-wrapped taffy and come in all kinds of flavors. The best thing about Kits is that they are only two cents, so for a quarter we can walk out of there with pockets full. It's December 28, 1969, and cold out, so we have big jackets on to hide the candy we are smuggling into the Forum.

My heart beats just a little faster, as I see the big, round stadium come into sight. The Forum is the home of the LA Lakers built just for them in 1967. The building was designed to remind people of the Roman Forum, but this is lost on me. I'm ten years old, and all I know is that important things happen in that building. I suppose that important things also happened in the Roman Forum, but today it's all about the Lakers. I can't wait to get in.

We climb those big stairs up to the top section. Those steps are so horrible and we have to sit so high. I hold onto the railing to keep from falling. I don't know it at the time, but Daddy helped build the Forum. He built those very steps we are climbing at the Forum.

We settle into our familiar seats, and we are making a mess with our Kits wrappers—unwrapping them and throwing them on the floor. We don't stay in those seats long because we want to get closer. Gary spots a few open seats down below, and so begins the constant seat-hopping around the stadium as we get kicked out from seat to seat not belonging to us. There's a trail of Kits wrappers to show where we have been.

We keep on moving. I just want to get a closer look. Lakers win 109-99 over the Celtics, and we head down for autographs. I want Happy's autograph, but more than that, I just want to be in his presence.

We finally make it down to the court, and there he is with all the other players. I'm holding out a piece of paper and pen.

"Way to go, Happy!" I yell, stretching my arm as far as I can and reaching out in hopes of his autograph.

He doesn't look happy.

"I'm not signing anything today," he says as he turns and walks away.

My heart sinks. I'm crushed.

He's a Laker, so I know I have to forgive him. But when I make it big, I'm not going to ignore any kids. I will sign as many autographs as they want.

While basketball is everything to us, I don't ignore other sports. Mama takes us to see the Dodgers quite a bit, and that spring I see big success on the baseball field.

I'm playing for the Compton Reds. I have a strong bat, and I play catcher and shortstop. I like playing baseball because Daddy can see me play on Saturdays when he is not working. I like the glory of shortstop, and while I like the control behind the plate as a catcher, I close my eyes when the ball is pitched. It's not until after I get hit with the baseball in a few games that I really learn how to catch.

I'm a standout and make the All-Star Little League team that season and go on to make the varsity baseball team as a seventh grader at Roosevelt Junior High School in Compton.

I think I'm big shit because I'm the only seventh grader to make the team of all eighth graders. Coach Barnes is my coach, and he is in such great shape. I walk around that big school like I own it. And I'm looking good in my uniform.

But in my eighth-grade year, I don't make the team, and who has time for baseball anyway? I do find time to meet up with my buddies to smoke weed. I smoke my first joint out on the baseball bleachers at Roosevelt Junior High School. It was never my plan to smoke weed. It just happened. Now, I spend my time smoking weed with my friends, and I land a job at Toots Liquor on Long Beach Boulevard. Daddy says it's important for us to have a job and help bring money into the house. I feel special because lots of people want to work at Toots, but I'm the one who got the job. This is a big deal and an even bigger deal than baseball.

I had never knowingly seen anyone do drugs before.

Years before, my Uncle Samalee came to live with us when he got out of prison. I walked into the bathroom and saw him sitting on the toilet, putting a needle in his arm. It was my first experience seeing drugs, seeing that needle in his arm. But I didn't understand it at the time.

"Mama, Uncle Samalee's putting a needle in his arm."

I just know doing drugs is bad because Mama and Daddy kicked him out of the house after that. And I know now that I don't want to mess with needles. So, smoking weed doesn't seem so bad. At least I'm not sticking a needle in my arm. I know I need to stay away from that liquid drug my uncle was using.

I will never do what you do.

Those words will become big in my life. I watched others make the wrong choices with drugs. I'm smarter than all of them. I know what I am doing.

At least I have a plan for which drugs to stay away from.

Chapter Five

One day of practice is like one day of clean living.
It doesn't do you any good.
—Abe Lemmons

Now that I've put my baseball career behind me, I'm playing lots of basketball with my brothers out at South Park in Compton.

We hang out there a lot, and there's this little building in the park that we call the "party house." I go into the party house and smoke a joint while Dennis and my other brothers are playing ball. I don't let my brothers see me. If they see me, they will beat me up.

I'm playing basketball, smoking dope, and working at my new job. I only smoke like a couple joints a week.

I'm working at Toots Liquor Store on Long Beach Boulevard. I'm only thirteen years old, and I have a job to go to every day after school. This makes me feel like I'm a little better than the rest of the kids. It's the one thing that helps me stand out in my family—I want to be successful and I'm going to start early in building my career.

After school, I walk real fast to get there on time because I don't want to disappoint Vern. He's the owner, and he's real good to me. He's a bald-headed white guy, and I look up to him because he has a successful business. I'm interested in learning everything there is to learn about running a liquor store.

Toots Liquor is located in a strip mall with an Orange Julius, a dry cleaner, and a Laundromat. Its large red letters spell out Toots Liquor for all to see. I'm proud to be a part of the store. Toots is the place to go in the neighborhood.

I work hard for Vern, keeping the floors clean and stocking the store. We get big deliveries every Thursday, and I move fast to get the boxes unloaded and stamp the prices on the bottles with a big ink gun. I have a system—I cut the box open with my razor and stand over the box like I'm shooting each one of the bottles.

Bam. Bam.

Each one of the bottles gets tagged with a black ink number, marking the price.

I work real hard when he's around—I want Vern to like me. He even says he's going to help me get a car. He tells me I'm a big part of the success of the store, and he gives me the important jobs to do. He's cool, too; he carries a gun and always has lots of money. I like being around this kind of success.

Mama and Daddy work really hard, so I know what hard work looks like. I don't want to be a cement mason like Daddy, though. That's tough physical work, and Daddy's always trying to drum up side jobs on the weekends to make some extra money. Daddy wakes us up on the weekends, telling us to get out of bed to help him with the side jobs. He's always telling us that if you don't work hard, you'll end up with a hard head and a soft ass.

I really don't mind hard work, but I'm thinking that there's a smarter way to earn money. I'm making my own money, and soon I learn about how to make some extra money on the side.

I work with these three sisters from Alabama—Dorothy, Mary, and Betty Jean. Anything you need to know about a liquor store from bagging groceries to stealing wine—I learn from them. And, they are teaching me how you can steal and not get caught.

"See, here, Karl. All's you gotta do is ring up the stuff on the addin' machine," says Dorothy.

I'm mesmerized by her big lips. She and her two sisters have these big old lips, and I'm watching these lips as she tells me how you can make some money by not even running it through the register.

We are all a big family in Compton, taking care of each other. Dorothy has all these kids that she doesn't know what to do with, so I offer up my little sister, Renee, to help out. Renee is Mama's right-hand, helping with the household and with all the little siblings. She's one tough cookie, and she can certainly handle it.

Renee's not too happy with me, offering her up to help with more kids. But she does it. She even takes those little kids with her to softball practice—she's got two in the stroller and the other little kids are helping to push them down the street. Renee is strong-willed and determined. She's so much like Mama.

I'm making like twenty-five dollars a day on the side in addition to my actual paycheck. I'm making so much money, but so is Toots Liquor, so I don't feel that bad. Vern knows something is up, so he takes me down to take a lie detector test. I am nervous that he is going to find out about the money I've been taking on the side. The thought of letting Vern down makes me sick.

Vern tells me that he's not supposed to take me for a lie detector test without my parents' permission, but he takes me down there anyway. Vern's been so good to me, and I don't want to let him down. I figure I can go down there and tell a lie and get away with it.

I fail the lie detector test.

"You failed, Karl, but I wasn't supposed to take you down here for the lie detector test without your mama knowing. So, we are just going to throw that lie detector test in the trash."

I can tell Vern is a little mad, but he likes me. I do a good job for him, and he takes good care of me, promising me that he'll help me buy a car and hooks me up with a source to buy weed. Daddy's not too fond of Vern, and he's really not fond of me getting a car.

CHAPTER SIX

They say that nobody is perfect. Then they tell you practice makes perfect. I wish they'd make up their minds.
—WILT CHAMBERLAIN

DADDY TELLS US that you can't play ball if you don't get passing grades. In fact, we are not allowed to play sports unless we have the grades.

"You can't be good at ball, if you can't get good grades," he says.

We don't see him a lot because he works all the time. He leaves the house at four in the morning and gets back at eight at night. I don't talk much to Daddy because either he's working or I'm working. I know what is expected of me, and I do it because I don't want any trouble with Daddy.

I make the C basketball team as a freshman at Dominguez High School. This is all based on what they called "exponents" such as my height and weight. Lil' Red is a senior and is all smiles when he makes the varsity basketball team at Dominguez High School. He is the last to be picked for the team, but he doesn't care.

The C team travels with the varsity team, so I can see Dennis play. He's my older brother, and I look up to him. I know that he's an excellent ball player, but Dennis is not getting the playing time he deserves.

After one of my games late in the season, I shower and dress and join Dennis at the end of the bench, where I sit for my duties as the ball boy for varsity. We are playing against Compton High School, and there he sits at the end of the bench again. I'm getting mad because Dennis is a solid player—he works hard and he deserves time on the court.

"Why is the coach not putting you in?" I ask.

I'm averaging about thirty minutes of play, but Dennis is lucky to get in for a couple of minutes each game.

"Shut up, Karl."

I know that Dennis doesn't want me complaining about his lack of playing time. I just don't understand why the coach is not playing him. But what I really don't understand is why Dennis is not pissed off about it.

"You're the last guy to get off the bench," I continue.

Dennis is not listening. He's watching the game. I can't focus because I'm just so angry—I'm even more angry that he's not mad.

We get home that night from the game, and Dennis heads back out to the park to shoot. But I don't understand why he's doing that. The only way he's going to get better is to get in the game and get playing time.

He walks back in the house about nine-thirty.

Just shooting the ball is not going to get you better.

I think it and know better than to say it.

He's tired, so I keep my thoughts to myself. He's always practicing, and he's never getting in the game. This is crazy.

We go on like this all season, Dennis playing one minute of the game. I am so disappointed for him because I know he is a good player, but he is an even better person. He's not getting the respect he deserves.

That summer, I am invited along with two hundred LA-area kids to the Jerry West Clutch Basketball Camp. This is a big deal. Coach Harris, who coached both Dennis and me at Roosevelt Junior High School, nominated me.

I'm so excited because Jerry West is huge in basketball. He is an NBA legend known as "Mr. Clutch" for making big plays at critical moments in the game. But I'm not thrilled about leaving my family for a week. At fifteen years old, this is the first time I will be away from them for an entire week.

Mama takes me to downtown Los Angeles, where we meet in the parking lot of a bank to get on the bus to camp.

I'm nervous, seeing all these kids. I get out of the car, and I'm just standing there in my Chuck Taylor All-Star Converse shoes. They are gray and handed down from my brothers. Because of my place in the Johnson line-up, I rarely get anything new. Shoes are shoes, though. Mama never throws any shoes away. Thankfully, basketball is a cheap sport—just need a ball, some shoes, and short pants.

I look up, and there standing by the bus is none other than Willie Naulls. He played in the NBA from 1956 to 1966, concluding his career with the Boston Celtics.

"Hi, Margaret," he says to Mama, and he gives her a hug.

Willie Naulls went to San Pedro High School with Mama. He played for UCLA and went on to deliver a solid NBA career. And he's calling Mama by her first name.

I'm so nervous, but I feel like I'm meant to be here. Our bus arrives at Harvey Mudd College, one of the eight colleges collectively called the Claremont Colleges. It's just about thirty miles or so from downtown LA, and will be our home for the next week. We are staying in the dorms, and the food is unbelievable. We get these great big old breakfasts, lunches, and dinners. Mom always fed us good, but I'm telling you, I'm amazed by the food—there's just so much of it.

On our first day, we get divided into ten-man teams. My buddy, Michael Bilberry, is on my team and we have Nolan—he's our big gun. Nolan has this shot that is a killer. We quickly figure out a system, and I do a lot of cherry-picking. When my team gets a steal or rebound, I'm at the other end of the court ready to get the long pass and score. I cherry-pick like twelve points a game. I am the cherry picker, and it works.

Now, I sort of know that cherry picking is frowned upon. It's not illegal, but I get the feeling that it is not respected. I don't care because it works, and we are winning.

Camp Clutch is amazing. Not only are we eating like crazy, we get to swim and work out all the time. We are having mean pillow fights in our dorm rooms. I'm a professional pillow fighter—have to be with all the people in my house.

Each day we get on vans to travel to the different gyms for drills. We never leave the colleges. We get on the vans and travel from gym to gym.

I am picked to do special drills with Jerry West. I'm not nervous because I know what I'm doing.

"What do you think your best and easiest shot should be?" Jerry West asks the group.

A bunch of kids reply, "jump shot," and I'm thinking the same thing, but I don't say anything because I'm standing on the court next to Jerry West to help with the drill. I feel like I'm his assistant and not just one of the other kids.

"Lay-up. You need to think about a lay-up as your easiest shot," he says. "If you can get a lay-up, you should never shoot a jump shot."

I'm thinking this is big coming from a guy who was known for his jump shots.

He puts a chair in front of the basket and tells me to stand on it. He throws the balls to the kids and tells them to make a lay-up around me. I put my arms up to defend the basket and brace myself to be knocked down. Amazingly, I am not crushed to the ground and now I am justified in my cherry-picking because I go for the lay-up every time I cherry-pick the ball. Jerry West said you should always go for the lay-up.

Nolan and I are picked for the Camp Clutch all-star team to play in the championship game. But the team we have been playing on all week also makes the championship, so Nolan and I have to play against our own team.

Dennis and Mama come to watch me. Mama goes to every game for us kids—sometimes going to four games a day just to see a little bit of each of our games. Mama's my rock—she does so much for us. I can count on her to always be there. I don't know how she does it, working full-time as a counselor with Head Start. We all went through Head Start and learned our numbers and letters to get ready for school—Mama knew how important early education was, and she made sure we all had access to it. She loves us all, but there's only one of her and there's lots of us.

I'm looking up in the seats to see Dennis watching me on the court during the championship game. I want him to be OK with my basketball. I need his approval and guidance. We are victorious, and I'm headed home with two big trophies, even though Camp Clutch wants me to stay for another week. I want to go home to be with Mama, Dennis, and my family. And what I really want is to smoke a joint—a full week here with no weed has been a struggle.

Chapter Seven

Some people want it to happen, some wish it would happen,
others make it happen.
—Michael Jordan

Mama and Daddy are not getting along so well. Daddy is a hard worker, but he likes his drink. Being a cement mason is hard work. He gets his coffee in the morning and heads out to his truck. He pours gin in his coffee cup and goes off to lay brick. He's what we call a functioning alcoholic. Years later I will understand this. Daddy is chasing demons like we all do.

Daddy grew up in Texarkana, Arkansas. He knows hard work. He shagged golf balls and shined shoes for ten cents at the nearby country club. His daddy, my Grandpa Herbert, left his family to find work in California and then sent for them to join him four months later. Daddy, his mama—my Grandma Minerva—and his two little brothers took a train from Arkansas to Barstow, California. My Daddy's aunt cooked them seven bags of fried chicken, a little bread, and some hot sauce for the journey. When they arrived, they saw Grandpa Herbert drive up in a new, shiny Cadillac. Daddy knew this was a good sign—Grandpa Herbert found himself a good job in California. Daddy would eventually drive a Cadillac, too. He always drove a Cadillac—but an older model because he had a lot of mouths to feed.

There was opportunity for them all in California. They lived in the Banning homes in East Wilmington. This is where the blacks lived, coming to California from the South—Mississippi, Alabama, and Arkansas. Daddy wanted to work in construction because that's where the jobs are. He taught himself to read blueprints that had been thrown away and became a cement mason—solid work, but hard work.

Daddy has always known hard work and by the time I'm in high school, it is really taking a toll on him. After going out drinking on Saturday nights, he comes home in a foul mood most of the time. Mama takes the brunt of it. It scares me to see him raise his hand like that. She doesn't do anything to deserve this. She deserves better for going to work, raising the kids, and taking care of the home. I hate to hear her cry. Charlie tells us to make a circle around Mama to protect her. We are prepared to help Mama when he comes home from a night of drinking.

Daddy is a Korean War Veteran, and he has earned honor for his service. He works hard to feed his family and make sure all us kids have what we need. There's honor in that, too. Daddy's not a bad man. He just likes his drink.

Mama can't take it anymore, so it's time for her to move to San Pedro to live with my grandparents. This isn't the first time they have split up. Mama was so young when she married Daddy, and then Daddy was sent off to the Korean War. Mama was lonely without him and ended up getting pregnant by another man and having three kids—Marion, Kenny, and Jimmy. And Daddy had a kid with another lady—his name was Kenny Dias, which is kind of confusing because Mama and Daddy would go on to have more kids together, and now we have two brothers named Kenny. Mama and Daddy divorced during this time, but they were meant to be together, so they remarried after the war.

But Mama can't be with Daddy right now with all this drinking and hitting. She leaves with all my siblings, including Dennis. I don't leave because I have a car, a girlfriend, and a job. I'm the only one who stays behind with Daddy. I'm scared of him, but know how to stay out of his way. I want my independence to do my thing, and Daddy's so busy with work that he doesn't pay me much attention.

Besides, someone should look after him, and it might as well be me.

After high school, Lil' Red tries to enroll in Compton College to play basketball, but he is told that he is not good enough to make the team. He's not giving up and continues to play basketball all over Compton, Long Beach, and San Pedro. He's playing recreation leagues, and he is coached by Charlie with no legs and grows five inches that year to six feet four.

Vern stays true to his word and cosigns a car loan for me so I can buy my first car. It's a 1964 Chevy Impala. It's tan and has Cragar wheels—the rims are so shiny. I can't afford the hydraulics, so I have these springs in the back and every time I put on the breaks, the back end bounces up and down. I'm in the tenth grade at Dominquez High School. I'm so cool.

Daddy doesn't approve of my car because I am only fifteen years old, so I park it around the corner on Harris Street and ride my bike home. I don't want Daddy to know about the car because he will be so mad. Harris Street is on the other side of Long Beach Boulevard in another neighborhood.

My best friend, Kenny Johnson—not to be confused with my two brothers named Kenny—lives in the neighborhood where I park my car. I go visit him quite a bit, and one day I'm parking my car and here comes this beautiful girl coming out of his house.

"Who is that?"

"That's my cousin, Sherry. Do you want to meet her?"

That's how Sherry Johnson becomes my first girlfriend. She is so pretty with dark brown skin and long black hair that she wears in a ponytail. She's well-built and a little bit of a tomboy. She doesn't let any of the boys touch her, including me. She's a neat dresser in her bell bottoms and tube tops. But, what really drives me to her is the fact that her last name is Johnson.

If we get married, she doesn't have to change her name!

There's a group of us who hang out on Harris Street, just around the corner from my house in Compton. Sherry's friend is Leah King and they are ace buddies. Sherry's brother, Calvin, goes out with Leah. We think we rule the neighborhood.

Sherry and I cruise around Compton in my Impala, bouncing up and down at the stop signs, singing to Blue Magic.

"...let the sideshow begin. Can't afford to pass it by; guaranteed to make you cry..."

I'm singing right along because my voice is so high that it works.

"...hurry, hurry step right in..."

I love these guys. Their voices are just like mine.

Later in my tenth-grade year, Sherry doesn't want to go out with me anymore. I catch her on Harris Street in my car—since I have to park it away from Daddy—with another guy!

I pull him out by his hair and beat the crap out of him.

In my car with my girl!

I'm playing JV basketball with hopes of moving up to varsity the next year. I don't know anything about setting goals. I don't know that this is something that you do. I live in the moment—in the here and now. All I know is that I love basketball, and I love the money I'm making at the liquor store.

I'm smoking weed a lot and missing more and more of school. Big Red and Lil' Red are starting to get on my case about it, but I'm not listening. My craving for weed takes over my mind. It is all I can think about, and I'm just having a good time. It's the 1970s—smoking weed is what everyone does, anyway.

At least I'm not like those poor winos who hang out in the alley next to the liquor store. I can't stand to see them get the shakes, so I take care of them. A little booze to take the edge off and they pay me back by giving me the scoop on the street. They know what's going on out here—it's important to get this information, and it doesn't take me long to realize that I can make some money selling weed. I'm selling and smoking weed. I pay $125 for a pound of weed and turn it into $325. I smoke about fifty bucks of it and pocket a hundred and fifty dollars. Not a bad turnaround, and I'm having some fun with my friends.

I don't see Lil' Red much anymore with him living in San Pedro and working out all the time.

I rarely go to school anymore, and I only see my brothers and sisters twice a month. I very seldom see Daddy because he is working all the time.

Lil' Red enrolls in LA Harbor Community College after Coach White sees him playing in a recreation league, and he goes out for the basketball team. He makes the team and averages about fourteen points and seven rebounds a game. He's only six-feet four inches, but his wingspan is like that of a seven-footer. His hands are huge.

He meets a girl named Donna Davis at LA Harbor College. This is his first real girlfriend, but Dennis doesn't bring her around us much. She comes from a real nice family and is a little different from all of us.

Dennis has found a way to get on that court, and I'm finding my way around the streets.

Where there are drugs, there is violence. I get my first gun. It's a twenty-five-caliber automatic, which makes me feel stronger than everyone else. I buy it on the streets for fifty dollars. I'm fifteen years old.

I don't have that gun very long. One day after school, I'm out in my driveway flailing the gun around, acting like I own the world. The cops come around the corner and set their eyes on me. I panic and throw the gun in my backyard, but they see the whole thing. They go in the backyard and get the gun. I'm busted. I get charged, and I go to jail for the first time.

Possession of a weapon.

I have to wait in that Compton jail until Daddy gets home. He comes down to the jail to get me. He is pissed, but he doesn't hit me. I thought for sure I had it coming. I am so relieved—I am scared of Daddy. He's a strong man.

I am barely going to school, and I can't keep up with my craving for weed. I am stealing more money from Toots Liquor so I can buy weed. It is a hunger that I can't quite satisfy.

This hunger is ruining my ability to go to school—I can't quite keep things straight.

My junior year at Dominquez High School is a wasted year. Daddy and I never see each other, which is a good thing because he is not thrilled with me. I know that he tells Mama that my job at Toots Liquor Store and Vern are my problem. Mama is not happy, either, and she says it's time for me to move in with her in San Pedro, so I can get back on track. I start my senior year at San Pedro High School, and it is strange because 95 percent of the student body is white.

I want Mama to be happy with me. She's such a good person and she deserves good kids. For Mama, I'm going to get myself back on track. I make a decision to scale back my use of marijuana—something that is easier said than done.

Thankfully, I make the varsity basketball team, and I have a strong season, earning an honorable mention all-league. I get a job at Helbert Auto Sales, and I find that I'm a good salesman, convincing folks that the cars on our lot can't be beat. The problem is that there are not a lot of customers. It's slow and I get bored, so I quit the job at Helbert and go to work for Uncle Herb at his liquor store. Uncle Herb is Daddy's youngest brother.

Uncle Herb—named after my grandfather—owns King's Liquor on Pacific Avenue and Santa Cruz. We are the kings in the neighborhood, selling the legal stuff. But as in any neighborhood, the liquor store is the connection for all vices.

Since my brothers have lived in San Pedro for a while before I get there, they have this town figured out. It doesn't take me long to get connected—and drugs are everywhere. I am back to smoking weed and playing ball with my brothers.

Leland Park is the spot where it all goes down. Dealers come to serve, and I notice that more and more people are smoking PCP. I just stick to smoking weed for now. My brothers have friends who deal, but they tell them to leave me alone.

My oldest brother, Charlie, is like the general around here. He graduated from college with a degree in recreation, and he runs the Teen Post, a place for all of us to go and play ping pong. Charlie has such a big heart, and he has taught us brothers so much—he even taught us to swim even though he can't swim himself. He is such a positive force in the neighborhood. He arranges for us kids to go to the LA Rams football games. All we have to do is bring a lunch and a little money to spend, and Charlie gets sixty tickets for kids in the neighborhood to go to the game.

We live in a place called Park Western—in the government "projects." I feel like I'm just living in one place after another. I still don't like moving and am not happy we ever left our house in Wilmington.

"Don't mess with Karl. He doesn't need any of that," my older brother, Kenny, says to his friends dealing.

After basketball season is over, I see no reason at all to continue to go to school. I'm so far behind in my credits anyway. I drop out of high school, but so what? I have a job and skills that other kids don't have. Mama is not happy with me, but I'll show her. I'm going to be a successful businessman.

I'm a high school dropout, but Dennis is enjoying his finest year of basketball at LA Harbor Community College. He's on fire and is considered the best community college player in California. His team wins the state championship. The game is in Fresno, California, at Selland Arena against Compton College for the Community College State Championship. Lil' Red scores thirty-nine points and has ten rebounds—he is named the Community College Player of the Year.

So, he gets the last laugh. Compton Community College didn't want him, so he showed them by leading LA Harbor Community College to win the state championship.

I'm so proud of him. He got little to no playing time in high school, but he kept at it. He made it happen for himself. Maybe shooting all those hoops after dark really did pay off. I can't help but feel a little jealous that he gets to play ball and I don't.

I hang around the local San Pedro parks, getting high with no direction or goals. My family is hounding me to get my high school diploma, so I enroll in community college and take night classes two days a week. I'm bored, and I quit going.

My life is all about working at the liquor store and getting high.

Lil' Red gets two scholarship offers—one from Pepperdine University and one from Azuza Pacific University. He chooses Pepperdine University in Malibu, California. We go and see him play—here's this black family from Compton going to Malibu to cheer on our brother. It is quite a sight, but they all like us because Lil' Red is a good player. And Donna is always there—she follows him everywhere. I get along with everybody, but I get the feeling she doesn't like me. She doesn't talk to me, barely even looks in my direction.

On our way to Pepperdine to see Dennis, we stop and get some food for him. He's on scholarship to play ball, but doesn't have a lot of money for food and living. We stop off and get buckets of chicken for him. We know he is short of money, so we all pool our money together and give him cash when we go to see him play at Pepperdine.

Dennis is playing and studying around the clock. He is moving fast in the basketball world. Things are happening, and he is playing good for the Pepperdine Waves. I get to go with him a couple of times and see that he has now become head and shoulders one of the best players in the area. In fact, the scouts are watching him. They are at pretty much every game now.

One day, I'm hanging out at the flagpole at an elementary school in San Pedro. That's where everyone meets up. The cops show up.

"Let me see your ID," the cop says.

I pull out my wallet and open it up. There is a joint in there.

"What's that?" he asks, as he pulls it out.

"I don't know what that is," I say.

Here we go—arrest number two, but it's my first arrest for drug possession. I get thirty days, and do fifteen days in Los Angeles County Jail. I heard that LA County Jail was tough, but they are softies. I can handle this. No big deal.

I'm not playing ball anymore. I actually stop playing for a while. I'm focusing on just getting high.

I get a DUI coming from work at King's Liquor. It costs me a hundred and fifty dollars, which I take care of because I am earning good money working at the liquor store. Two weeks later, I get another one, and now the judge sends me to traffic school. This time it costs about $900, which is much more difficult to pay.

Dennis is shining, and he helps the Pepperdine Waves get a good start in the West Coast Athletic Conference. I'm still getting high all the time, but Dennis is on the move. He is playing so well and helps the Waves get into the NCAA playoffs, where they upset the University of Memphis in the second round, 87–77. They meet up with UCLA at the Pauley Pavilion in the regional semifinal, but they lose 70–61.

Dennis is all over it. He played great and there were scouts at that game taking notes. Now, I'm beginning to wonder if Dennis will have a chance of reaching his dream of playing in the NBA.

CHAPTER EIGHT

Any American boy can be a basketball star if he grows up, up, up.
—BILL VAUGHN

DENNIS IS GETTING calls from the NBA. There is one team that is really hounding him and another that's telling him if he continues his education, they will make him a part of their team the next year. It's our hometown team, the Lakers, telling him to finish his education.

One of the teams that is hounding him finds a rule that allows him to be drafted if he decides to enter the draft. He enters the draft as a hardship case in the 1976 NBA draft. The NBA had a rule that players were not eligible to be drafted until their four years of college eligibility was up. This rule was challenged in court in 1971, and the player who challenged the rule won. Hardship cases could now enter the NBA draft—lucky for Lil' Red.

I'm listening to the draft on the radio. I can't believe it. My brother is in the NBA draft. Then I hear it with my own ears.

Lil' Red is drafted in the second round by the Seattle SuperSonics.

He did it. One of the Johnson brothers made it to the NBA!

I'm so excited for him and feel like he is finally getting the respect that he deserves. Dennis never gave up—he is proving that hard work gets you places. My mind is racing with thoughts of our pact and how we are going to take care of each other when one of us makes it big. Dennis made it, which means I made it because that was the pact.

Dennis is now a SuperSonic and signs a four-year contract. He is offered $60,000, which is $45,000 plus a $15,000-signing bonus.

Mama and Daddy are back together, so they get to celebrate the news of their son's success together. After Daddy's drinking caught up with him and he did eight months in LA County Jail for multiple DUIs, he never had another drink again. With the alcohol out of their relationship, Mama and Daddy were able to get back together.

First thing Dennis does is buy a house for Mama and Daddy. This is consistent with the plans we made in our bunk beds as little boys. Dennis buys a house at Ninety-Seventh and Budlong Avenue—not far from the Forum. It's a beautiful four-bedroom, two-bath home with a swimming pool.

The ink isn't even dry on Dennis's contract when Donna discovers that she is pregnant. Dennis wants to make it right, so he marries Donna before he heads up north. This is a surprise to all of us. We don't even know about the wedding until the last minute. Mama tells us all to get dressed and get to Dennis's wedding.

Wedding? What is he doing?

That summer, Dennis plays in the summer professional league, where he shines. He averages fifteen points a game his first professional action. He is ready for the big time, and I can't wait to be a part of it.

This is the other part of the Big Plan. If Dennis makes it in the NBA, I get to go, too.

"What do you mean I don't get to go?"

What is he doing? We had a plan. We had a pact. When one of us makes it—our group is taken care of.

This is what we waited for our entire lives—we talked about it. We made plans for what was going to happen when one of us hit it big. Well, he hit it big, and I'm supposed to go with him. Gary and Renee get to go. But he's telling me I can't go.

"Karl, you have to get your shit together."

I know that Donna is the real reason I don't get to go to Seattle. She doesn't like me, and she doesn't like my lifestyle. She is taking my brother away from me, and Dennis is turning his back on me. He has changed.

Months later, she loses the baby. That will be their only shot at having their own children—they eventually will go on to adopt three kids.

She stole my brother from me.

His first NBA season is shaky. He is playing back-up and averages about nine points a game. Life isn't great for me living with my parents. Daddy and I do a lot of hollering at each other. The yelling matches are about me sleeping all the time. I'm getting high and sleeping. This is what I have to do to deal with my brother turning his back on me.

My brother just made it in the NBA and abandoned me.

Daddy eventually convinces me to go to work with him, and I do. This is hard work. I'm helping him lay this brick and decide it's time to try night school again because I need that diploma. I don't like disappointing Mama and Daddy—they are hard workers. I want to do the right thing, but I'm finding it harder and harder to do these days.

They work so hard to provide for their kids. I owe it to them to go back to night school—again. I only need five credits to earn my high school diploma. Going back to school turns out to be a good thing because that's where I meet Jana. Her mother is one of the instructors, and Jana is a teacher's aide. I like her the minute I see her, and she quickly becomes the center of my world. I find that I need her in a way that I have not needed anyone before. She is the girl of my dreams.

Things are good with Jana, and she is teaching me about a lot of things I never knew about. She grew up in Huntington Beach, not far in miles from Compton, but a world away, and she surfs. I think this is so cool, so she teaches me how to surf. She takes me out to restaurants, which is new for me. I never went out to eat at restaurants except for McDonald's, and that doesn't count. We go to a Chinese restaurant, and she orders all this food. I'm wondering how we are going to eat it all and pay for it. We walk out of there with cartons of leftover food. I'm just amazed by the experience; she seems so sophisticated ordering from the menu and paying the bill. The thing with Jana is that she knows how to take care of business, and I decide this is the kind of life I want to live.

I earn my high school diploma in 1976. I decide to follow in Dennis's footsteps and go to LA Harbor Junior College. I want my brother to be proud of me. Maybe if I go to college and do good things, he will invite me up to Seattle, so I can be a part of his NBA career. The coach said he would give me a shot at trying out, since I am Dennis's brother. I surprise myself by making the starting five. Things are going well as I begin my junior college career. I average eight points a game, and I even have a couple of nineteen-point games. I'm still getting high, but I'm able to control my addiction.

During summer workout, Dennis comes home from Seattle and plays summer ball at LA Harbor College as part of his workout program. I'm so proud. This is my NBA-professional-basketball-player brother. He is playing with me and my team—what a thrill.

I start the second season at LA Harbor College, but I don't get too far. My coach thinks I have the world's worst jump shot and tells me to stop shooting jump shots. He tells me if I shoot another jump shot, he will take me out of the game. The pressure to perform is mounting because I want to be as good as Dennis. You would think the coach would give me a break because my brother plays in the NBA, but it's the opposite—there is a higher expectation for me.

I'm going to school during the day, playing basketball, and working six days a week at the liquor store. We sell the legal stuff in the store, but there's the illegal stuff in the back room. I have spent years saying no to the cocaine, but one night after I miss eight jump shots, I try cocaine for the first time, snorting it. I get such a rush. Weed never made me feel like this. It's like I'm flying, and I can do anything. This is exactly what I need to help me play better. At first, I snort coke only a couple times a week.

In no time, the feeling is so good, I can't stop at just a couple times a week. I feel like I can take on the world. My brother is a professional basketball player, and I have a great job and a great woman. Things are really good.

We are playing against El Camino Community College, and I'm coked up. I'm feeling strong because my brother is an NBA player, and I belong on this court. I go in and shoot a jump shot, and it goes in. I look over at the coach and smile as if to prove that he was wrong. He still takes me out of the game.

I'm thinking I'm real smart and that no one knows I'm using cocaine. I am wrong. My coach dismisses me for breaking team rules.

As Dennis arrives in Seattle for his second season, he is all business. There is some shake-up on the team. Head Coach Bill Russell stepped down after last season's performance. But his replacement, Bob Hopkins, doesn't get the job done early in the season, and the Sonics lose seventeen of the first twenty-two games. Hall-of-Famer coach Lenny Wilkens takes over, and Dennis earns a starting position. Dennis just takes off in this role. The play-by-play announcer Bob Blackburn starts to call Dennis "DJ" because there are two other Johnsons on the team at the time—John Johnson and Vinnie Johnson.

The Sonics make a trade for our boyhood idol, Gus Williams, giving them a backcourt that is considered by most experts to be the best backcourt in basketball.

Coach Wilkens pairs up Dennis and Gus, and things just start to click for them. They are amazing the second half of the season. I have been watching Dennis on TV and finally get a chance to visit him in Seattle during his second season. I've been waiting so long for this, and I can't wait to be a part of his NBA career. I feel like I have been shut out for too long.

My brother Kenny and I drive his Toyota Celica to Seattle. It is a horrible trip because it's December and the weather is bad. We finally get to the home that Dennis and Donna bought in Bellevue, Washington. We have to take the ferry over to their house. It feels like a world away. They have a very nice house, but honestly, I thought it was going to be much bigger. My brother's an NBA player and the house doesn't match his level of play.

They put me up in the basement, and right away, I don't feel welcome. Donna doesn't want me here, and she has all these rules. We have to get all dressed up for the game, and she wants us to go straight home after the game and go to bed. I don't want to do that. I want to go out, drink beer, and have some fun. She really doesn't like me being around. Too bad, though. I want to be with my brother and cheer him on.

Kenny has been here many times and knows the Seattle area really well. He has a girlfriend named Sheree that he met, and Kenny knows the scene here well.

I'm amazed by the pace of life here—Dennis and Donna are on the go. I go to Dennis's practices before I even go to a game. This is a little like getting the behind-the-scenes access. It is the best thing in the world to go to an NBA practice. I can tell Dennis's confidence is up—they were so close last season, and he has work to do. He's starting off-guard with Gus running the point. Dennis has this look in his eyes—it's the look of a champion.

I'm in the bleachers watching one of the practices and see Gus Williams sitting on the sidelines eating Famous Amos cookies. That's a big surprise to me to see so many players sitting out practice for one reason or the other. But, every time I come to practice, Dennis is practicing. He was disciplined as a teenager, and he is still disciplined.

I'm DJ's little brother, and I feel like I belong here. I'm family, so I'm entitled to some of the perks, so I ask Gus Williams for his shoes. They have the greatest shoes, and he's not bothered by me asking. Besides, I can make great money selling those shoes and all the autographs that I grab.

I only go to two games at the Kingdome. I enjoy the practices more, because at the games, I have to sit next to Donna. We just can't get along. We do it silently and don't make any scene about it. The seats are incredible. Front and center about four rows up. I just can't sit next to her.

After one of the home games, I go with Kenny to meet his girlfriend, Sheree. She has a friend named Randi. We hit it off, and Randi takes me to see the underground party scene in Seattle. I'm just doing lines of cocaine. We have a great time.

As I head back home, I feel kind of bad about my time with Randi. It is actually the first time I cheated on my girl, Jana. But I'm not living with Jana yet, so I feel justified. I was getting high the whole trip and just having a good time.

Shortly after I come home, I move in with Jana in Long Beach in a small apartment. Things are kind of going good on the surface, but I am hiding an addiction problem. I go back to King's Liquor because I like the energy of working at night. Now I am spending most of my nights at the liquor store, while she is working during the day. We spend Sundays together and go to the movies a lot. There's a movie theater close to our apartment, so we walk. We are not accepted in Long Beach, though. Jana's white, so her walking down the street with me is a problem—it's a problem for everyone else. We get harassed by the cops quite a bit.

We are headed to the movies one day and get stopped by a police officer. He asks for my identification. I'm really mad because there is no reason that he should stop and question me. He takes my license and asks me a few questions about where I live and how long. They are just stupid questions.

He's not satisfied by my answers, but he's running out of questions. He realizes that there's nothing he can do about a black man walking with a white girl to the movies and lets us go. Long Beach is not the right place for us, so we end up moving back to San Pedro.

I am the assistant manager at the liquor store, and hide my drug use pretty well. I am running the business, and I'm making good money, but I am starting to borrow against my paycheck to get drugs during the week. When I get my check, I am usually short like seventy-five bucks. I lean on Jana to figure it out because she's good at paying bills. She always comes up with a plan on what we need to do. She is a perfect human being and I don't want her seeing me using drugs.

One night, I'm watching game four of the NBA Finals at the liquor store. We have a little TV in the store just to the right of the cash register on a little shelf, and it's always on because Dennis sometimes gives King's Liquor Store a little plug.

"I'd like to give a shout-out to my brothers at King's Liquor," Dennis says to the TV camera.

My work at the liquor store is getting sloppy. I can't really focus on my job, anyway. I'm just planning on how I'm going to buy cocaine. Eventually, the drugs win and I lose my job.

Now I can focus on my new full-time job—selling cocaine. I'm hanging around the projects in Wilmington and enter the drug game full-time. Now my job is selling drugs. Rock cocaine is new on the scene, and for whatever reason, I try it and I love it. It is cocaine mixed with baking soda cooked up until it is hardened—crack. This is good stuff. You put it in a pipe and smoke it—the high is out of this world.

But then I come down, and now I need it more. It's so expensive.

How am I going to get the money so I can smoke more crack?

The Sonics continue on to win the Western Conference, where they come up against the Washington Bullets and Elvin Hayes in the 1978 NBA Finals. It's a great back-and-forth series that goes to seven games. Seattle had lead in the series and

Washington had come back to tie it. Dennis comes into game seven not complaining, but physically hurting and goes 0–14 from the field—probably the worst game of his career, and Seattle loses by four points. He broke his ring finger on his left hand, but didn't tell anyone. He just played through the pain.

I hit the streets and up my game. Dennis is also upping his game. As I watch him on TV, I can see that Dennis has that look in his eyes again. There's no stopping him. He's sinking shots left and right, and I'm so proud of him. I feel like I'm walking on the clouds. His defensive game is getting the attention it deserves. His ability to block shots and get the rebounds is unmatched.

The 1978–79 season will see some revenge. Dennis will more than make up for his scoring drought in the 1978 NBA Finals. Dennis has made sure that he will not let his performance in the 1978 NBA Finals shadow this year's performance. He is named NBA Final Most Valuable Player and makes his first All-Defensive First Team and All-Star Game appearance.

Time is lost when you live in a fog. I clear up my head enough to track Dennis's performance on the court. But I can't shake these feelings of abandonment and jealousy.

Chapter Nine

These are my new shoes. They're good shoes. They won't make you rich like me... They'll only make you have shoes like me.
—Charles Barkley

Dennis is on the NBA radar screen now. I don't talk to him much, but when I do, he seems very edgy. He's frustrated with his pay. I read in the newspaper that Coach Wilkens called him a "cancer" and that it was apparently Dennis's time to move on from Seattle.

Whether he is liked or not, his defensive game is on fire and he enters contract negotiations. Dennis is not getting the respect he deserves. Just like it's been his entire life—his talent is not being recognized. He's patient, but I am not. It's like I'm sitting on the high school bench with him again, telling him that he deserves more.

Dennis is so much better than they give him credit for.

He gets traded to the Phoenix Suns. Even if all the sports reporters don't admit it, I think that he's the most underpaid player in the NBA at $65,000 a year. He is a bargain contract. Talks are rough, and I can see the effect it is having on my brother. Although his game is not suffering, he has become really moody. He doesn't want to talk to me because he doesn't want to hear how much the NBA doesn't respect him. He's slipping away from me. And I continue to slip.

I manage to get back to my job at the liquor store, but my addiction is getting worse. I hide it well from everyone except a few people. I am a working addict who does not know how to stop using.

Jana and I have been living together for more than a year. Things have been going well, and to be honest, even though we are living together, I don't really see Jana all that much because of our work hours. She is still working days, and I work nights.

I hardly see Dennis while he's playing for the Suns. He is busy shaping his career, taking care of his family, and getting used to his new Suns teammates, whom he leads to the Western Conference Semifinals two times during his three seasons there. He earns his only All-NBA First Team appearance and is voted into three consecutive All-Defensive First Teams. He is at the top of his game and makes two All-Star appearances while in Phoenix.

Dennis is a force at big guard. He's finding success on the court, and I don't get to be a part of any of it. But I don't care anymore because all I am doing is sleeping, working, and getting high while Jana is at work. Jana is solid and exactly what I need to help me keep everything straight. She doesn't even drink alcohol, let alone do drugs. But I think she needs to loosen up a bit, so I convince her to have a drink with me once in a while.

I am completely absorbed with myself, my drugs, and spending money like it grows on trees. During Dennis's first season with the Suns, Jana and I take a trip to see them in Phoenix. Jana and I really need to spend some time together. We finally have a whole weekend together, and we drive down to Dennis and Donna's. We make the six-hour drive from LA in Jana's Honda Civic.

They live in McCormick Ranch, a beautiful subdivision of luxury homes in Phoenix. It's a big, gorgeous home with a swimming pool. A much bigger home than they had in Seattle. I'm so proud to bring Jana with me, and I'm excited because whenever I see Dennis, I get shoes and sweat suits. They are also giving us a TV for our apartment.

We get there, and Dennis comes out with this little TV. I'm so pissed. I'm thinking: You make all this money and you can't do better than this TV? It's old and small. Donna makes Dennis do the dirty work. I know that she put him up to giving me this pathetic TV. She has a possession over him. She can have him doing anything.

Why the hell are they giving me this TV? She hates me. Why isn't Dennis taking care of me?

I'm so mad that I don't even want to stay, so I put the lame-ass TV in the trunk and tell Jana it's time to go. We are arguing all the way back.

"How embarrassing. You acted like a jerk. They were giving us a TV, and you are mad that it's not big enough. What is wrong with you?"

Jana is going on and on.

"Why don't you understand why I'm so pissed? We drive all the way out here for that damned TV, and it's some lame hand-me-down piece of shit."

I'm yelling because she doesn't understand. Dennis was supposed to take care of me. It's a long drive home, and I need a fix bad. Now I know why I don't spend much time with Jana anymore.

I am paranoid that she is sleeping with someone else and just go crazy on her. Once the fighting starts, we can't stop.

The fights, yelling, and arguing get worse. I am threatening her because I know that I'm losing her. She gets a restraining order put on me, and she slips out with all of her clothes and belongings while I am at work. It was a well-planned move, and everybody knew about it but me. Even one of my own friends helped her move out. It was them against me. And I know her mother is behind it. Jana can't make a move without her mother's approval. It drives me crazy because her mother controls her every move. Jana can't walk through the door without her mother telling her to walk through the door. I know that her mother told her to leave me.

At least I don't have anyone controlling me now. Five years is a long time to spend with someone. I tried to play it tough, but I'm torn up. I won't let anyone see it, though. I'm distraught at the thought that I don't have anyone to take care of things for me.

I jump on a bus headed for Phoenix. I need to see my brother. I don't call Dennis to let him know I'm coming because I know what the response will be. When I arrive, I don't go to their house. I don't want to see Donna—I can't face her judgment of me.

"Take me to the Suns stadium," I tell the cab driver. "I'm going to see my brother."

Just saying the words make me feel better.

"Oh, yeah, who's your brother?"

"DJ"

"With the Suns? No way! That's awesome, man."

Yes, it is awesome. And he's going to take care of me.

I show up unannounced at the Suns stadium. Nothing makes sense, and I'm so messed up.

I just have to tell the guard that I'm DJ's brother, and they let me in and put me in a small room. DJ walks in and stares at me with my suitcase in my hand.

"What are you doing here?" he says.

"I've come to see you play."

"You can't stay here."

"Come on, Dennis, I just want to see my brother play."

"Karl, you have to get your shit together. You can't be here. Look at you. You are a mess."

His words sting. Deep down I know that I'm out of control, but these feelings are too painful. I have to mute the pain. I take the money he gives me for the bus ticket home and head to the local park, where I know I can find what I need to dull this pain of rejection.

I'm all alone.

I find what I need, but it's not long before a cop comes up on me. Busted. Arrested. The cop takes me down to the police station to book me on drug possession.

He asks me where I'm from and why I'm here.

"I'm visiting my brother."

"Well, who's your brother?"

"Dennis Johnson."

"What does he do? Can you call him?"

"He plays for the Suns."

"DJ? No way."

The two cops are just smiling at each other. I can tell they are trying to figure me out and if this is for real.

"Well, I know DJ I'll just give him a call," says the fat cop.

He thinks I'm nervous about him calling a professional basketball player to come bail me out.

Go ahead and call him and you'll see. Dennis Johnson is my brother.

Next thing I know, the two cops come and get me.

"It's your lucky day, Johnson," says the fat one.

"Turns out your bro did come," says the other one.

It's about three a.m. The police station is not buzzing with people. But there is a buzzing in the station among the cops. I walk past the desks and turn back to look at something on one of the desks that caught my eye.

There's a basketball on the fat cop's desk. I make out a scribbled "Dennis Johnson" that is still glistening wet—fresh autograph.

I smile. Not because the fat cop got a signed basketball and because I got bailed out. I'm smiling because my big brother came for me.

Dennis puts me back on the bus to LA.

CHAPTER TEN

I'm tired of hearing about money, money, money, money, money. I just want to play the game. Drink Pepsi, wear Reebok.
—SHAQUILLE O'NEAL

I AM ON the run most of Dennis's third year playing for the Suns, but it doesn't click that what I am going through with my addiction is hurting other people. I'm so absorbed in this drug world—I am using 24/7. It's costing me more than my freedom—it is costing me my ability to move forward as a man and better myself. I suppose the only good is that drugs make me forget about the negative effect on my family. I'm going deeper and deeper away from reality; and, frankly, I really don't care. All I care about is getting high, and that's what I'm doing.

Mama gets so mad at me, but she doesn't give up on me. She pulls out her Bible and quotes scripture.

"God will let you know when it's time to get yourself right," she says.

One day, I come by her house so strung out that I'm acting like such an idiot. My little brothers are there, and she starts to scream at me to get out of the house.

"Get out of here, Karl. You get away from your brothers!"

She's in the kitchen washing dishes and her finger is pointing at me, dripping soapy water. Next thing I know, she picks up a pot and throws it at me.

Fine. I'll go.What's the big deal?

My sense of reality is off, but I'm able to focus enough on what Dennis is doing on the court. His 1982 season is possibly his best season. It is the season that they win the Pacific Division. The Suns team is built with two strong guards, a powerful front line, a pretty good center, a rebuilt bench, and all the motivation to win an NBA championship. By taking first place, the Suns get a first-round bye, and the players are well rested when they face their second-round opponent, who also is trying to get back to the finals—the Lakers. A better team than the Suns could not have been put together for this match-up.

The Suns won the regular season series, but this means nothing in their quest for the championship.The series goes bad for the Suns, and they are swept by the Lakers. It is all bad. Dennis plays a really good series, but in the end, it was not enough, and he shoulders most of the blame. I suppose that someone had to be blamed, so why not blame the guy that made all-league? Dennis does not accept this blame too well—he knows he did his job.

I turn off the TV in the liquor store. I'm a little pissed by the Suns' missed opportunity to grab the championship. I'm just hanging out like I always do at the liquor store—this is where all the action is. The phone rings, and I pick it up.

"Hey, fool, you Johnson?"

"Yeah. Who the hell are you?"

"I'm gonna shoot up your punk brother!"

Phone goes dead, and I go into action. I'm still fired up about Dennis losing the championship, and I'm ready for a fight. I grab a gun and head out. I'm not sure where I'm going, but I start running up the hill toward Mama's house—I have to get to Lyle to warn him. I'm a little crazed—no one messes with my little brother. God knows that my older brother Dennis has already been jerked around.

I see the reflection of the red and blue lights on the slick pavement before I hear the siren.

Shit. The cops.

I put my arms up.

"Before you get up on me, I got a gun," I say.

There's two of them, but it feels like an entire army with guns pulled on me.

"Drop your weapon!"

"It's in my front pocket."

"Drop your weapon! Drop it now!"

They can't hear me, but I don't dare move. They are getting closer.

"My front pocket!"

They are finally up on me and take me to the ground. The cuffs are on, and I'm back in jail.

Mama comes up with a plan. She's a really good thinker.

"You know what we're gonna do? We're gonna find you a drug program," she says.

We find the drug program and convince the court that this is the best path for me. I get a court order to the program. Even Dennis comes back to help convince the judge that I need professional help. I'm so thankful for him coming back to help me. If the judge doesn't want to listen to me, I know he will listen to Dennis. He's an NBA player—and a great one at that, even if they blamed him for the championship loss to the Lakers.

It's really a wonder I am not dead. I have been in and out of trouble for so many years. This time I have high hopes—it is finally my time to get clean. Like Mama said, God would let me know when it's time. And it's time.

Sure enough, the judge listens to Dennis and orders me to the drug program. It's my golden ticket out of my legal troubles. Dennis is the one who takes me down to Riverside to the residential drug program called My Family Incorporated.

"What are we going to do when I get out?" I ask Dennis.

He's taking care of me. My all-star brother is taking care of me.

"We'll cross that bridge when we get to it," Dennis says, as he will say to me many times.

I arrive at My Family Incorporated in Riverside, California. I'm doing really good in the program and make it to nine months sober. I feel great—never realized what kind of fog I was living in. It's like I was underwater for years—muffled sounds and sights. Even the food tastes better.

I'm good at this recovery stuff. I'm in charge of the fundraising committee, kitchen committee, and even the discipline committee. The discipline committee is my favorite. If one of the patients breaks a rule, my discipline committee will determine his or her punishment.

There's this one lady who is acting like a real witch. She's mean to everyone and just talks bad to the others. So, I determine that she needs to put on a witch's hat and pretend like she is riding a broom around the room. That will fix her attitude problem

She's pissed, but she does it because we are the discipline committee and she has to or she's out of the program. There is a staff member who serves on the committee, and the program condones this punishment—it is peer discipline and meant to expose the patient's shortcomings.

We have these rules, and if you break certain ones of them, you can be discharged. If you are court-ordered to be there, you really don't want to be discharged for your behavior. This is bad, because the court will give up on you forever after that.

After nine months of being sober, I'm progressing really fast. Then the little snag happens. I am accused of leaving a cigarette burning in an ashtray, which is against the rules.

So, now it's me coming up against the discipline committee—*my* discipline committee.

Cindy, a white lady who has been sober for ten years, sits in my position as chair of the committee to dole out my punishment. She's a beautiful lady who has the respect of the entire place.

I'm feeling good about this because this is my committee and they have already given a pass to another patient who did the exact same thing.

"Karl, you know that leaving a cigarette burning in an ashtray is a dischargeable offense, right?"

I nod.

Where is this going?

"This program is about breaking old behaviors, and leaving a cigarette burning in an ashtray is not only irresponsible, it is part of your drug habit."

They just gave Dave, the white guy, a pass. Why are they making such a big deal?

"Yeah, I know. I don't know why I'm here for this. You just gave Dave a pass for the exact same thing."

It comes out a little more defensive than I want, but now I'm mad, and I start to argue with Cindy that they are making this into something it's not.

This is not fair.

My discipline is to put on a "baby diaper" and get into a crib for an hour a day. They say I'm acting like a baby, and they want to break this behavior. It's part of this special therapy—behavior modification. I doled out the "witch" therapy, and now it's my turn to do the "baby" therapy.

I'm really pissed now. They hand me this sheet and some safety pins to put on like a diaper. I'm told to get it on and climb into the crib.

There was a time when I wanted to be the baby—Mama's baby boy. When she brought my little sister, Renee, home from the hospital, I threw a fit. I ran out into the yard, telling her to take that baby back.

I'm still the baby. I want to be the baby.

I just don't want to be the baby now.

This is bullshit. I'm not doing this. It's a double standard. Dave, the white guy, got a pass for leaving a cigarette burning in the ashtray. The black guy has to put on the baby diaper and get in the crib. This is humiliating.

I quit.

Renee comes and gets me. She doesn't say a thing. I'm pissed about how I am treated.

I never liked the program anyway. We go straight to the courtroom the next day.

"I want to make you do some more days," the judge says. "But you got a good report every three months you came in, so I'm going to give you time served."

I got out of that program and didn't finish the after care. I thought I was clear.

I got this—nine months' sober—I nail it.

It doesn't take me too long back on the streets to realize that it is the drugs that will eventually nail me.

Chapter Eleven

One man can be a crucial ingredient on a team,
but one man cannot make a team.
—Kareem Adbul-Jabbar

It doesn't take long to slip back into my drug habit, and I suppose it will be just a matter of time before I lose my job at the liquor store.

I am living back at home with my family in Palos Verde, and it's uncomfortable because I am using, but using less because there is no way that I could use at my family's home.

Dennis purchased this home for my parents in 1980, and it's in a very upper-middle-class neighborhood of the Harbor area, so I can't come to terms with doing drugs in this house. So I have a plan: every four days, I leave looking for a job and go to a couple of places and spend the rest of the time getting high. It works for about two months, but then I find Mama in the front room crying one day when I get home.

"Karl, what are we going to do with you?"

"What are you talking about, Mama?"

"You know what I'm talking about. I will never give up on you, but I just can't stand to watch you waste your life."

She's sobbing. I can feel her pain, and it's a shot through my heart. So many feelings wash over me—regret, despair, shame. The tears come because of the pain I have caused Mama.

"Maybe it would just be better if I was dead."

"If God wanted you dead, you would be dead already."

While I'm worrying Mama with my drug habit, Dennis is worrying all of us with his basketball troubles.

I'm having a hard time tracking Dennis's career, so I start writing it down in a notebook:

> *Season started with trade rumors circling all around Dennis and you could tell it was a season that he was really bothered. His points per game dropped from 19 to 14, and in a way it was just getting him ready for what would be his next test. I think the Suns made the playoffs, but they don't do well. But still, if you graded the trade, Dennis would win. He took the Suns to three straight playoffs, but that was it for Dennis and the Suns. Dennis was shipped to Boston, which would turn out to be the worst trade to date in the Suns' history. Dennis to Boston for Rick Robey and a draft pick that summer. Dennis told us, his family, on a phone conversation that there was an investigation going on in Phoenix involving some players, and that his name was mentioned, but that he was clear, but the Suns needed a scapegoat, so he was sent to Boston. I asked what the inquiry was about; he simply told me he was advised not to talk about it. Clearly, I knew now he was immersed in politics of big-time basketball. Anyway, apparently there was a player from the Suns who was hurt in a car accident and there were drugs involved, so the whole team was questioned. I guess not talking about it made it go away.*

Dennis has a couple of cars down in Riverside, and he asks me to drive one to Boston. This is an opportunity to do something for him, and I'm thrilled that he asked me. He gives me $500 for my time. The night before I'm supposed to drive the car to Boston, I go party. I've got $500 burning a hole in my pocket. I end up in jail again for drug possession.

I let my bro down. He asked me to do one little thing for him, and I couldn't do it. As I'm sitting in that jail cell feeling sorry for myself, I wonder why I couldn't do it. I blame the drugs—I'm not in my right mind, but is there something else that blocks me from helping him?

He never came back to LA after the trade. He went straight to Boston for a press conference, where it was revealed that the Celtics general manager had been after him for years. Apparently, Dennis was the missing piece to their championship puzzle. It's good to see my brother arrive in Boston with a big smile. He even has a surprise for me in the off-season—Dennis, Donna, and their son are now living down in Riverside, California, in between our mom and Donna's mom, who lives in Barstow, California.

I am getting deeper into my addiction, but I'm starting to make some money selling drugs. I don't have to ask anybody for money anymore. I am living a life on the run—always moving from hotel to hotel. I am not sleeping very much. I am seeing a girl named Darlene. She is also using cocaine and something else that I suspect to be heroine. But I don't have time to focus on her addiction. I am too busy with my addiction to worry about someone else's. I pick up a case in 1984 and got a little jail time and probation, which I know I cannot meet because I am using and having to drug test. I seem to be slipping, but it doesn't seem to bother me because addiction has a funny way of not letting people see reality. I am making bad decisions and headed to nowhere while Dennis is building a strong career with the Celtics. I am happy for Dennis and the Boston Celtics.

I really am happy for him.

I'm a player on the streets. I'm testing the rules and even writing some of my own rules. I've been in and out of court and jail so many times that I know how to work this. I can't always go in as Karl Johnson, so I try out a few aliases to keep me in this game. I jaywalk across the street in front of a cop

"Hey, what are you doing? I'm going to write you a ticket for that."

Go ahead. That's exactly what I want you to do.

He asks for my identification, but I don't have any. So he asks me for my name.

"David Burns."

I show up in court as David Burns for the jaywalking ticket. Now David Burns is legitimately in the system.

Bingo. That was easy.

Sure enough, a couple of weeks later, I get pulled over for speeding.

"Man, I don't have any ID on me, but I just got a jaywalking ticket like three weeks ago."

The cop goes back and checks it out. He comes back with a speeding ticket for David Burns.

Bingo again.

"OK. Get out of here and go pay your jaywalking ticket."

Now the system thinks I'm David Burns. This keeps them at bay and hides the fact that I have a warrant out for my arrest under the name of Karl Johnson.

I'm weaving a necessary web for survival in this criminal world. Joe Dodson is another alias I use because now I'm creating a long rap sheet for poor David Burns. It's enough to keep them guessing. Even I have a hard time keeping it straight sometimes.

CHAPTER TWELVE

If you are going to take it to the bank,
then you better cash it in.
—SHANNON FISH

I MAKE A name for myself on the streets. I'm known to the dealers as "Quick Karl" because I know how to sell cocaine quickly. My reputation is based on my ability to scout out the deal and turn the stuff into cash real quick. I'm making these guys thousands of dollars a week.

Not just anybody can enter this game. Trust is big. Dealers will only hand over their powder if they know the cash is guaranteed with a quick turnaround. There are only two ways to get into this game—you are born in a drug-dealing neighborhood or someone brought you into a gang.

I didn't have to go the gang route. The Johnson brothers are known on the streets. We have built-in credibility because we own the liquor store, selling the legal drugs—alcohol and cigarettes.

The white stuff is king, but it also doesn't hurt that my brother is DJ. If you are going to take the drug supplier's stuff and sell it, you have got to have the street cred behind it.

This drug game is all about flipping—making a profit. I spend fifty dollars and sell the cocaine for a hundred dollars. I set aside about twenty dollars, and smoke the rest of the crack. So next time, I'm walking in with seventy dollars and getting more powder to turn. This is how I build my business.

I work from six in the evening until about six in the morning. I make most of my money in the early morning hours. No overtime pay. You got to do what you got to do to make the sales. I don't care about any overtime pay—I'm getting what I need to feed the monster, making sure I get my fix every day. But, I don't show that I'm using to my dealers. This is a sign of weakness, and I will not show them any cracks in my armor.

My eyes are fixed at the end of the street, ready for my customers to come around the corner. I know their cars, and even if I don't know the car, I know by the way they are driving that they want to buy. I walk from corner to corner, ready to jump to make the sale. On a good week, I'm making $10,000 for just one of my dealers—hand to hand. I'm moving quick.

If it's one of my regulars, I jump in the car and he drives down the street; then he drops me off. I may or may not get into the car—depends on how busy the street is, and if I know the customer. I trust my gut. This stuff is so in demand that I'm making deals left and right. If I can avoid getting into the car, I do.

There are creative ways for customers to get this drug. The street is marked with holes in the fences, where they can snatch the cocaine through the fence.

The customers are needy—it's a crazy need that may call for desperate action. I know after four or five deals whether customers have the money or they are a little short. I understand this insane need for the cocaine. If I know that a customer is a little short on cash, I'm not going to show him all that I have.

It's how this drug game is played. My dealer controls how much I get, and I control how much the customer gets. It's my little way of keeping control. I know that cocaine is the one in control.

I feed the need little by little, so they keep coming back. It's just like any good business with a good product—keep them wanting for more.

One of my favorite dealers is Wes—he's also known as a "baller" for his efforts to maximize profit on the streets. Wes has a great big sack. He buys about $35,000-worth of cocaine at a time. This gets him two keys of cocaine. Then he mixes it up with baking soda to blow it up to double its size—called a double-up—and cooks it to make the hard substance.

Now I take the double-up and go flipping.

Both keys produce about fifty-six ounces of cocaine together—I pay Wes $1000 an ounce, and I can flip that into $2000, but I smoke $500 of that. When I come back with more money to buy from Wes, he knows I'm doing good. He's turning a profit of about $20,000—not a bad flip. My flip is not that much because I'm using.

Wes is a good guy. He's a country boy from Arkansas and quit smoking dope when he came to California. He realized that there is lots of opportunity to make money here in East LA—dope comes in easy from Mexico. He's building a really good business and travels back and forth to Arkansas, buying up lots of land with all this money.

He builds a really good drug business, and he takes care of his crew. We even go out to eat for a nice meal in a restaurant at least once a month. Sort of like employee appreciation dinners. You got to take care of your people—this drug business is no different.

I'm one of Wes's best runners, so he wants to be sure I'm taken care of. He has taken me under his wing and tells me how to be. I listen to him.

"Karl, you don't have to go out there and act like a thug. This is a business, and you have to act like a professional to be successful."

One day Wes takes me to The Sports store and pulls out wads of money. He buys me some really nice clothes. A month later, he even buys me a Volkswagen Karmann-Gia coupe.

This is a fantastic way to live.

I take pride in my appearance because I take my job seriously. Wes teaches me that as a professional, I need to set the tone for my deals.

And I have other things to worry about. I can't let my brothers and sisters see me all grimy. I don't want them to run my life anymore.

I'm running my own life, and I'm making good money. Wes may be my favorite dealer, but he's not the only one I'm flipping for.

My career is really taking off. I'm in demand and not bound by a territory because I'm not a gang member. I can go to any neighborhood to work—I can do Compton, Wilmington, San Pedro, and any neighborhood in between.

I know the Bloods. I know the Crips. They are not territorial with me. I'm not bound by any allegiance—I am a free agent. They know me as a ball player. They don't know that I'm sliding in selling drugs. To them, I'm a ball player. That's my cover.

On any given day, I have dealers hunting me down to sell their product. My biggest problem is that I am using along with selling. Dealers are coming out of the shadows to get me to move their stuff. Now I have leverage, and I'm playing one against the other.

I'm on the run because I owe people money. I don't like owing people money, but my addiction is getting more demanding. I'm using too much. I'm losing my grip on reality and having a hard time keeping it all straight.

This is dangerous, so I have to keep two motel rooms—one where I lay my head to sleep and the other one to do my serving. I'm smart. I never tell anyone where I lay my head. Sleep is not something I do often. I stay up for days—most of the time I'm staying up ten days in a row. Just keep on running, selling, and using.

The cocaine keeps my body going. I feel like I could go on forever. But then my mind starts playing tricks on me. I think I'm seeing things, and now I'm losing track of my money. I think people are stealing from me. I just can't keep it straight.

"You go take rest," one of my dealers, Javier, says in what sounds a little like English with a heavy Spanish accent.

I'm like a caged animal—I can't stop, so I don't take a rest.

I sell $10,000-worth of Javier's stuff, but I owe him $500. I'm doing a really good job hiding from him because I know that he will shoot me for just five dollars.

I'm hanging out in the Junkyards in Wilmington with my best friend, Lety. The Junkyards are also known as the "Third World." It's a bunch of junkyards with homeless people living in boxes across from the docks. The Junkyards are where we do our business. Customers drive along Foote Street, and that's where we do our business. It's like a cocaine drive-thru. I can always catch them coming.

Lety has my back. She is a lesbian Mexican girl, and she always has beautiful women hanging around her. I let her stay with me when I have a motel because she's a good friend, and I don't mind hanging out with beautiful women.

She's a tough one with a short and stocky build. Several years back, I got into a little scuffle where this guy pulled a knife on me, and she stepped in the way of it—she got cut just a little. Lety's a stud, and she's got my back.

It's about two o'clock in the afternoon. I'm standing in the middle of the block along Foote Street, and I'm watching both corners for my customers to come around the corner. Lety is just down the street on the other side. I hear the loud pipes of a Ford truck barreling down the street behind me. As it passes, I see a blur of Javier in the driver's seat.

Shit. He saw me.

He flips a U-turn.

"Here we go!" I yell to Lety across the street.

Javier gets out, along with another Mexican guy I haven't seen before. My fists are already up. I'm ready for a fight—I'm known as a fighter, and I'm good at it. Here comes Lety—she's like my Mexican insurance. But even she can't make Javier back down.

Javier approaches me. He's a little guy.

"Don't worry. I got your back," Lety says as she stands next to me.

I know Javier has guns, but I'm thinking he's not going to kill me. I make him too much money.

He's not going to pull a gun on me.

My fists are up.

"You have money?"

"I owe you money, but you not getting it now. I ain't got the money right now. I'm working on it."

I'm stammering now, and I don't like how desperate I sound.

He's closer now—I'm ready to throw my punches.

There are no punches. Just a gun he pulls from the front waistband of his pants. I think my heart skips a beat, and it's pounding now in my ears when I see that gun. I hear the gunshot over my heart pounding in my ears.

He shot me!

Then there's another shot. His companion shoots me. I'm in shock.

"You're too quick! You no run no more!"

I hear him over the pounding in my ears. My legs are throbbing and burning. I'm on the ground, and Javier is standing over me pointing the gun now at my face.

"No pole-lease! No pole-lease!" Javier is yelling.

Don't shoot me in the head.

I think my eyes are squeezed closed and when I open them, I realize that Javier is gone.

Lety is yelling. I can't hear her. They shot both my legs, and now I see the blood.

"Come on, Karl. Get up."

I can't get up.

It's in the middle of the afternoon, and we have to move quickly. We can't run the risk of the police showing up. Lety drags me to the end of the street, to the corner of Foote Street and Anaheim.

An ambulance shows up. Not sure who called. No one has any phones out here.

Lety's flagging down the ambulance as if we are hailing a cab.

They take me to St. Mary's Hospital in Long Beach.

"My legs! My legs are burning!"

I had never smelled burnt flesh before, but I know what that smell is now. It is my own burning flesh, and it smells so bad. I end up at St. Mary's Hospital with two gunshot wounds to my legs. The doctor is taking a look as a police officer comes in.

"Mr. Johnson, who shot you?"

"I don't know."

I'm not talking. I do tell him that I was sitting at a bus stop and got shot in a drive-by shooting. I can tell that he knows I'm not telling the truth. He's got a lot of rounds to make in this ER, so he doesn't waste his time with me.

The hospital discharges me, but I'm still in so much pain. Javier's shot to my left leg entered the outside of my thigh and exited the other side. The other shot that came from his companion went into my right calf—I asked if the bullet was still in there, but I don't think I got an answer. The answer will come soon enough.

Mama and my sisters are crying.

Karl got shot!

My brothers are just pissed. They think I deserve it for being mixed up in this world, selling cocaine.

Back at Mama's house, I pull off the bandage around my right leg, and there's something sticking out of the wound. I pull it out; it is a piece of metal from the bullet. Mama calls the hospital, and they say to come back down.

I'm not going back to that hospital.

In addition to the scars, I have what looks like a tumor the size of a golf ball on my right calf.

Much later, doctors explain that the bullet is lodged in my calf muscle.

I rest up at Mama's house for about a week, but I can't stay here long. I'm using, but I do not use at Mama's house. Mama knows me and she knows I'm using, but she's so supportive. She never judges me. I just can't stay here because coming off of cocaine sucks. My legs still hurt real bad, and I'm so sick just lying in this bed with my body screaming at me for cocaine.

"I just don't know what to do for you, Karl," Mama says.

I can't stand the sadness in her voice.

The drugs are calling me personally and professionally. I have to get back out there. The drugs—and the urge to use them—are more powerful than any gun.

I get such a rush from smoking and snorting cocaine. There are times when I don't have any to use. The calling to go out and get some is overwhelming. It's an agitation with no common sense. This is my motivation. I have got to work, and I have to feed the monster.

I'm right back at it. Lety and I go back to the Junkyards, where I got shot. She missed me and has been a little lost without me. She is truly my best friend in the drug world.

I'm holed up in a trailer with friends who I know I can trust. Javier sends a message to me that he wants to talk to me.

"Javier says: 'tell Quick to come talk to me,'" says the Mexican girl he sent with his message.

I am not going to go talk to the guy who shot me.

I ain't talking to him.

I suppose the good news is that street rules say that when someone shoots you, he is considered "paid." He's paid. He shot me, so I don't owe him anymore. That's the rules. If you get caught selling his stuff and he doesn't help you out, he is considered paid. If he comes to beat you up, he is considered paid.

He shot me, so he's paid. I no longer owe him.

The other rule that Javier knows is that if you shoot me, I shoot you.

But I don't play by this rule. I don't like guns, and now I'm really scared of guns. I've been so quick that I haven't had to deal with the gun thing. And I don't have money to pay for someone to shoot Javier.

This Mexican girl keeps on coming by. Javier's nervous. He's a Mexican who shot a black guy, so he's nervous.

I am finally convinced to go see Javier. I go to his junkyard, and he has all these guns lying around. I'm scared to death.

Why did I come?

"I try and tell you. You go lay down. You go rest. I pay for motel, but you no listen."

I can tell he's trying real hard to explain himself. He wants us to be even. We are not even. He shot me, and I no longer owe him. I have the upper hand.

"You take my stuff. You tell me you coming back. You no come back. We forget about all that, yes?"

I'm bulletproof now.

"You ready to come back to work?"

I like the leverage I have. He's the kingpin—he's got a big bag, and he's begging me to come back.

I agree to work for him again. He has a good supply, and I need the access. More importantly, I like the position I'm in now. Getting shot gives you more street cred.

I ease back in with Javier, only taking about $200-worth of stuff. Stuff I can sell in thirty minutes. I make $400, and I come back with his cut.

We are good now.

Javier has his insurance that I won't go to the police.

Sometime later, another runner owes him some money, and Javier shoots him in the head. Another dead runner who owed money. Javier gets caught.

I feel responsible. If I had taken care of my business like I was supposed to, that guy would not have gotten killed.

There are casualties in this war. I'm a good soldier—one of the best. Conning is my tool, and I'm good at it.

I am a heck of a fighter, and they know there are thirteen Johnson boys to back me up. So, I had back up.

I am a user. User of drugs. User of people.

My life is so dark. It's so horrible.

I see a pregnant lady walking down the street and she has money in her hand begging me to sell her drugs.

I hate them begging for the drugs with their pregnant bellies. It just makes me sick. I turn them down hundreds of time.

The worst thing you can have in this drug game is a conscience. I have a conscience and it is haunting me. I have to keep on snorting cocaine to numb my conscience.

Chapter Thirteen

Left hand, right hand, it doesn't matter.
I'm amphibious.
—Charles Shackleford

Dennis and I are not talking much anymore. I am in and out of jail. I do not know the damage I am doing to my brother and my relationship with him. I have lost my brother's trust.

What a place to be in life. I am so caught up in this mess. I'm on probation for one of my many run-ins with the cops. I'm not sleeping much, and I'm on the run because I had a dirty test—my drug test was positive, so now I'm in violation of my probation. Now I'm running from the cops.

I buy a 1976 Cutlass Supreme off the street from a guy who owes me. We make a deal for $150. I give him seventy-five dollars cash and seventy-five dollars' worth of cocaine. I'm driving the car around, and I notice that the brakes are pulling and making a little noise. I've got places to go, so I ignore my brake problems.

I see my friend, Keno, on the street, and he tells me that Priscilla is having her baby. Everyone looks up to Priscilla in the projects. She has a presence and demands respect. She serves, too, but not today because she's having a baby.

"Give me a ride to the hospital," says Terry, who's standing next to Keno.

I owe Terry money for a deal I did, so technically I owe him a ride to the hospital. Terry and Keno jump in the car, and we head to Kaiser Hospital in Harbor City, which is on the corner of Vermont and Pacific Coast Highway. I'm flying down PCH, and there's a car next to me that passes me on the right. As we approach the intersection to turn left into the hospital parking lot, the car on my right cuts me off and stops. I need to stop on a dime, but those brakes aren't doing their job. My foot is to the floor, but we are not stopping.

I am pressing the brakes all the way and turning the wheel to avoid hitting the car that cut me off. Now we are sliding into oncoming traffic on the highway. All I see is a big truck, and my Cutlass Supreme clips his tire on the driver's side. We are spinning, and the next thing I see is glass everywhere. Our car comes to a halt, and it's as if there is no sound. Like everything is in slow motion. I look over and see Keno slumped over the dashboard.

"Keno, wake up! Wake up! Let's go! We gotta get out of here!" I'm trying to yell, but it comes out all garbled.

Keno is not moving.

I touch my hand to my face and see blurry, red liquid all over my hand. I can't see clearly. It's fuzzy. Something is wrong. I'm bleeding, and I'm bleeding bad. But, I have to get out of here.

I have cocaine in the car.

I jump out of the car and run over to a bush and throw the dope in the bush. I look back to the car, and Keno is still in there. The guy in the backseat is gone, and the gasoline truck is piled into the gasoline station. He lost control and crashed into those pumps. The irony of a gasoline tanker crashing into the gas station is not lost on me, even though I'm in shock and out of my mind.

I start running and leave Keno there. This is bad. I have to get out of here. I feel someone grab me and tackle me. I'm like a caged animal, fighting to get out of here.

No, no, no. I can't see!

This person sits me down and tries to calm me down. There's just so much blood. I'm bleeding everywhere. Luckily, the accident happens right in front of the hospital. Next thing I know, I'm in the hospital and the doctor is putting his gloves on and putting his finger into my eye. Glass from the windshield is lodged in and around my eye. He takes his finger and cleans out the glass and moves the hanging skin around. I'm so tore up, my face is like hamburger meat, but now I can see.

"Mr. Johnson, we have to send you right into surgery to try to save your eye."

How does he know my name?

As they wheel me into surgery, there goes Keno walking out of the hospital. He acts like he doesn't know me. This is how our world works. We don't talk to the cops, and we don't give any information. I want to know how he's doing, but acknowledging each other would be a mistake. We can't give the cops any clues.

Good, he's alive.

The doctor saves my eye. When I wake up from the four-hour surgery, there is Mama standing over me, praying.

"It's gonna be OK, Karl," she says as she rubs my head.

She's my angel, and she's here to take care of me. She's always calm—I can depend on her.

Priscilla ended up having a big old baby boy. I didn't get to see the baby while I was in the hospital, but I was glad it all worked out for her.

Mama takes me back to her house in Rancho Palos Verde so I can heal. The doctor prescribes Tylenol Codeine for my pain, but I really don't like how I feel on this medication. It's different than the high I get from smoking crack—it makes me fuzzy, like I don't have any control. I have this great big patch on my eye like I'm some kind of pirate. Mama doesn't let me go anywhere. She says that I need to get my health right by going to therapy for my eye.

I'm bored to death. I have no patience for this healing thing I have to do. It's now four weeks after surgery, and no one is home. I go over to the hooks in the kitchen where everyone hangs their car keys. I'm popping the codeine pills, but what I really want is a beer. I take the keys to my Daddy's truck and head down the street. As soon as I put my foot on the brake at the end of the street, I flash back to the crash and my heart starts racing. I can't focus, and I'm breathing heavy. I pull into the parking lot of the grocery store, and it is all I can do to calm myself down enough to park the truck. I park way in the back of the lot away from the other cars because I can't seem to maneuver the truck. It's like it's driving me. I have no control, and I'm shaking so bad. Now, I *really* need a beer. I go into the grocery store to buy some beer, and I call Mama on the payphone. There is no way I'm getting back behind that wheel.

"Mama, I took the truck and I parked it. I can't drive, Mama—you have to come get me."

"Where are you at?" she's yelling.

"I'm trying to tell you. I'm down the hill at the grocery store, and I can't drive."

I don't want to go to therapy for my eye. I've got things to do. I need to get back in the game, and I need a fix big time. So, I go back to the bush where I stashed the drugs after the car crash looking for my dope. But it's not there.

Damn Keno.

I know that he went back there and got it. I had nothing but time on my hands while I was recovering, and I was able to capture some of Dennis's accomplishments in my journal:

So the 1984–85 season was a great year for my brother. He was truly playing good ball. He was winning games with his experience and knowledge of the games. He was healthy and also disciplined, and to be honest, I think that his family and his wife and kids were good. It was also a year that he had one of his finest basketball seasons. He was probably one of the top all-around guards in all of basketball and everyone knew it. He was just a fabulous player, and all his critics knew he would win championships. Another one to add to these other championships we already had from Seattle, where up to now he'd played his best basketball other than when he was with the team in Phoenix, where he was all-league first team offensive and defensive. He had reached the top, and I guess he had worked very hard, even as the core group of Celtics were getting older. Dennis was 31 years old, but also having an all-pro year and continuing to be one of the most popular and consistent performers of all time and continuing to make good decisions in his life with all that was going on. I must tell you, there are many decisions to make in a professional athlete's career, and his decision to take charge again on the court at the point position in the 1985 season was a big one and a decision the Celtics needed because they were having problems at the #1 position, but Dennis was focused and ready.

I finally leave Mama's house. I'm as good as I'm going to get, and it's time for me to start moving on. It's not long before I'm knee-deep in smoking crack again and motel hopping. I start bingeing because it's been so long—it's like I'm making up for lost time.

The bingeing messes me up real good. I'm seeing double, and it's not because of my eye injury. Then I start seeing things.

I'm sitting in my one-room studio motel room, studying the space below the door. I can see feet go by, and I'm counting those feet. I know how many feet are supposed to be going down that hall and when.

Wait. Who's there?

I see another set of feet.

Damn it.

My heart is racing now. I owe three dealers money. This robbing Peter to pay Paul thing is not working. Peter and Paul are getting pissed. I'm facing the door—I never sit with my back toward the door. Nobody ever knocks, so I have to be ready.

I have not slept for fourteen days, and I'm not even tired. I'm a working addict. At least I'm still getting up and going to work.

Dennis is coming to town to play the Lakers. I haven't had a chance to see him play in Boston, so I'm excited to see him in person with that green and white uniform, playing on what really is our home turf. We all go as a Johnson family to the Forum to see Dennis play as a Celtic.

What should be an exciting time turns out to be a horrible experience. Here's the simple truth: Lakers' fans hate the Celtics. We are all sitting there as the Johnson family—there to cheer on Dennis, but there's a lot of negative attention. Dennis is seen as a traitor.

"Hey, you red-head mother-f***er! Where did you get those freckles?"

I can't believe my ears.

Are they really yelling that at Dennis?

I look over to Mama, and I see the sadness in her eyes. We get through that game, but leave the Forum broken and saddened by this attack on us. It's just too much, and I never go back. I think that was one of the last games Mama went to at the Forum. It's too much for her too.

Even though I don't talk much to Dennis, I'm still tracking his career in my notebook. There's not a lot I'm keeping straight these days, but I need to follow Dennis's career.

> *His 9th season was solid and he was on top of everything. It was an Ironman season. He played 80 games out of 84 regular season games and again led the Celtics to a record home court win/loss and to the championship with a 41 and 1 record at home, which stands today as the best home record of all time. That team has been recognized as the best-assembled team of all time. What an honor to be one of the starting five: Larry Bird, Kevin McHale, Robert Parrish, Danny Ainge, at the two guard, and Dennis Johnson at the point. That team would win the NBA Championship that season again and the Houston Rockets and Hakeem O. and Ralph S., my brother would play a pivotal role in the series as usual and also have to go to blows with Sampson because he would never let a teammate go into battle by himself. What a teammate to have on your side.*

There are little perks to having a brother in the NBA, like getting free shoes. Dennis had a deal with Nike for a couple of years, but now he has gone over to Reebok. This is his first really big deal. He wore the Reebok Pro Legacy shoe along with Danny Ainge. He does a few commercials, including one with him and Danny Ainge in which Dennis "dunks" on Danny.

I try to get my hands on as many Reeboks as I can. I just call Dennis up, and he sends me some shoes. This is so cool. He gets about 125 pairs of shoes a year. And he gets all these sweat suits. He made it! This is the cool stuff that we knew would happen if one of us made it.

I'm living the good life with a famous brother, and I'm making a good living on the streets. I do find time to stay in contact with Mama and Daddy.

Daddy is sober—will be sober for the last ten years of his life. But now he has bone cancer.

I visit him every Saturday. After all the years of fighting, now we are really tight.

He is sitting in his chair in the house that Dennis bought for him and Mama. He is reading from the Bible, telling me about the verses that Mama reads to him.

Daddy is dying, but he doesn't tell me this. He just tells me about the Bible and that he now knows that he's going to heaven.

On this particular Saturday, I bring one of my girlfriends. Her name is Mary. She is real pretty.

"Well, who is this?" Daddy asks, looking at Mary.

I have different girlfriends and he's trying to keep up.

"You gotta be good to your woman, now," he says.

He's so small in his brown chair. The chair is like the cancer—eating him up. Daddy was always so strong, but not now. I can see how weak he is getting.

Cancer is ugly. It's ugly like an addiction, taking hold over you.

I am on the streets and I am so messed up, but I don't let Daddy see this. My business is thriving. I have a couple girls on the side who would do anything that I ask—that's why I'm bringing a different girl with me practically every Saturday to see Daddy.

I don't like to use the "P" word because I don't see it like that. It's a side business and you got to do what you got to do. But, really, drugs are the pimps.

"You comin' back next week?" Daddy asks, trying to be all tough about it.

"Yeah, I'm comin' back next week."

I came back the following week like I did every week. He finally decided to do the chemotherapy but he took one treatment and died seventeen days later. We bury Daddy at Green Hills.

"It's gonna be all right, Karl."

I'm standing at the funeral home in a line, as people I know and people I don't know keep on coming up and telling me that it's going to be OK. I am getting so mad. It's not going to be all right. My Daddy is dead.

"Why do I have to stand here and listen to all these people saying it's gonna be OK when it's not?"

"Do you need a little drink, Karl?" Mama says, which is kind of funny because she doesn't even drink or smoke. I'm so messed up that the alcohol can't even compete with the chemicals I've got running through my system.

"These are your Daddy's friends. Now just get yourself together."

"Well, they need to shut the hell up. Who are they to tell me it's gonna be OK?"

I'm not right. The drugs have a hold on me, but even they are powerless against the pain in my chest. I can't breathe. My Daddy is dead.

I thought he was going to beat cancer.

Daddy was a Korean War Veteran, and he was buried with honors. The US flag was draped over his casket. Daddy died at sixty-seven years old—just two years after he retired at sixty-five. Charles Lynn Johnson—all his brothers and sisters called him Lynn.

I'm living from motel to motel, running my business. My Uncle Herb checks up on me. Daddy's dead, and I go freaking nuts.

I'm like Daddy. I have an addiction, and I'm a hard worker. I'm a good person. I didn't want to be like Daddy. I wanted to be like Dennis. But being like Daddy has paid pretty good. My aunties take care of me because I'm so like my Daddy. They saw how good I was to Daddy, so they take care of me and give me money.

CHAPTER FOURTEEN

When you face a crisis, you know who
your true friends are.
—MAGIC JOHNSON

EVERY GOOD PLAYER needs a break. Running the streets finally catches up with me. I go to state prison for the first time at thirty-three years old. That's kind of late to go to prison for the first time for a guy like me. The difference between jail and prison is that in jail, there's no program. But in prison, you get to work off your time.

I know they are coming for me, and I am ready this time. I need a rest. That's what prison is for me—a little rest from this world.

It's no big deal, anyway. Level one security prison in Jamestown provides the quiet I need. I need a vacation. It was time to go to prison for a little break. I catch a two-year sentence and only end up doing six months. This is exactly the break I needed.

I'm not tracking Dennis very well. I'm busy with my own business. He is an assistant coach for the Boston Celtics, which is not a bad gig. He stays in that position for four years and is paid nicely until 1997. That's when Rick Pitino comes in as head coach and cleans house. Dennis is out of a job.

Dennis and Donna move to their home in Florida. I only talk to him a few times on the phone. I'm not asking for money anymore because I have my own money now.

I call him on the phone.

"What do you want, Karl?" He's edgy and snaps at me. He's taking care of three families—his family, Donna's family, and our family.

Later, I see it on the TV first before anyone can tell me what happened. There he is sitting in the courtroom in an orange jumpsuit. Being arrested is nothing new to me, but I can't believe that my hero is there in that courtroom.

Dennis must be stressed. What's going on with him?

He and Donna had a fight, and he threatened her. Their son called the cops because he was scared that his mom would be hurt.

The case doesn't go anywhere because Donna doesn't pursue it. The court orders Dennis to take anger management classes and to move out of the house. He moves into the building on the back of their property.

Our family doesn't talk about it much—just a little blip on the screen of Dennis's career.

Then, I catch a big one, and I don't mean a fish. I catch a case that will lock me up for many years.

I'm living in Wilmington with my girlfriend, Becky. Becky and I are such a good team.

I met her one day as she was beating up one of my friends over drugs. She's a tough white girl—a poor, white women's version of J. Lo. She's well-built and tough.

What the hell are you doing? Who are you?

I'm fresh out of prison again. And I'm huge. My arms are so bulky from working out in prison because that's the only thing going on in there.

"Why you beating up on my homegirl?" I say to Becky.

"Who are you?" she says defiantly.

"I'm Quick Karl."

"Who?"

That's the problem with being out of the scene for a while. There's a short memory of who's who on the streets. I'm anxious to get back in the game.

She runs off and goes back to the people she's working for. They come back looking for me with Becky.

I see her walking up the street with my friends, and she's pointing at me.

"Quick! When did you get out?" they say.

Now Becky's just looking at me with her mouth wide open. Her people know me because I used to serve with them.

"Do you want to work tonight, Karl?"

Hell, yes, I want to work.

"OK, you can work tonight with Becky."

With her? Why would I want to work with her?

She's good-looking.

OK, I'll work with her.

Becky and I are sent to a house where they are serving. My job is to watch the door. Not a bad gig for five hundred bucks. It's a good night. Lots of action.

"You're responsible for getting Becky back to the motel with the money."

I am?

I'm figuring I have about $10,000 from the night's profits. I drive Becky back to the motel in my new truck that I bought right out of prison. Mama told me to stay away from Wilmington because I won't get out alive again.

I'm back in Wilmington, and I'm back in the game.

I got this.

"Do you want to come over to my room?" Becky asks. "I got a room downstairs."

I'm taken off guard by her directness.

I'm attracted to her, and I have been out of prison for about a week. This proposition is well-timed. I go to her room, and that is the start of our partnership.

Mama doesn't like Becky. She's always telling me to get out of Wilmington and get away from Becky.

But Becky and I have something really good. We click. It's a good business partnership. She's tough, a good worker, and I am able to manipulate and intimidate her. She goes out and works, then comes home and gives me all the money. This is how this world is, and this relationship serves me well in it.

I knew love with Jana. This is not love, but it meets the needs to thrive in this drug world.

Time passes, and now we have been living together for five years in Wilmington. Mama still doesn't like me seeing Becky.

"Karl, stay away from Wilmington and stay away from Becky. You haven't gotten anywhere with her in five years."

I have a production assistant job in the City of Commerce. I'm on parole again for possession and sales of drugs.

"I know you too well. This is not going to work."

Mama is right. This girl will lead me back to prison.

On Valentine's Day in 2001, Becky and I are driving around and we make a deal with an undercover cop. She sells him about one-tenth of an ounce of cocaine.

Before we know it, we are surrounded by ten police cars directly in front of the Longshoreman Hall where two of my brothers work.

We both get arrested, and they impound my 283 Datsun ZS. I tell the cops that I picked up Becky, who was hitchhiking—that I didn't know she had drugs in her pocket.

I get released because I'm just the driver and my parole officer doesn't violate me by sending me back to prison. I run all the way home.

The next day, I'm driving down to the courthouse, and I can see Becky is on the bus, waving at me. I get to the courthouse and head up the stairs. She's walking out—she's been released!

How do you sell dope to a cop and get released?

What I don't know at the time is that there is a deal in the works for her to implicate me.

We continue living together in Wilmington, and for the next three months, I'm in the dark—until one day, I'm sleeping and she comes into the bedroom.

"There's someone who's been knocking on the door, but every time I open it, there's no one there," she says.

I'm irritated. She wakes me up to answer the door.

"I'll get the damn door."

I open the door and there are five cops standing there.

"Is Becky Miller here?"

Oh, shit.

I turn and look back into the apartment, and Becky's already at the window, trying to climb out.

They explain that her case has been refiled and they are there for Becky. Door is open and there's a foot in the door.

"No...yeah." I stammer.

I hesitate because it's obvious she's here—she's the one trying to climb out the window.

"Isn't that her by the window?"

They come in and get her.

Two of them take her handcuffed to the police car at the street. The other three stay.

"Now, are you Karl Johnson?"

"Yeah."

"We have a warrant for your arrest."

"For what!"

"Talk to your parole officer."

Apparently, my parole officer violated me because now she is getting a different story from the cops.

I'm charged with transportation of drugs—with transporting her and the drugs.

I'm in county jail for nine months, fighting the case. I resume my continual fight to get help. I have asked judges many times for a rehabilitation program during my many parades through courtrooms. I am always told I do not fit the program.

I write to Delancey Street, a drug rehabilitation program in San Francisco and ask to be a part of the program. They agree, but they will not come to court to testify on my behalf. I have to get the judge to sentence me to the two-year program.

I ask my public defender to help me out. I need her to convince the district attorney that I need this program. She has too many cases and doesn't have time.

Here we go again.

During the pretrial phase, Becky goes on the stand—I needed her to tell the story we had told the cops. The story that she was a hitchhiker and that I had just picked her up not knowing she had the drugs on her.

Becky takes the stand and pleads the fifth on grounds of not incriminating herself.

Damn it.

I'm now going to trial. My public defender claims that this is not going anywhere. I'm offered ten years, but I don't take it. I'm not guilty for what they said I did.

Becky and I take the same inmate bus, but she's in front of the cage where the women are and I'm in back with the men.

I move up closer to talk to her through the cage.

"What is your lawyer telling my lawyer?" I ask her.

"You need to take the three years that they offered you," she says.

"They didn't offer me three years. They offered me ten."

Sure enough. The offer comes down to three years. But if they came down to three years from ten, I'm sure there's more wiggle room. I didn't do what they said I did, so I'm not dealing.

So I go to trial—a jury trial of my peers. I'm realizing that the case is now not about the current charge. It's about my history and all of my episodes in and out of jail. I should have taken the three years.

I can't even take the stand to defend myself because if I do, I will do what they call impeach myself because I have three prior transfers-of-drugs charges.

But my good friend Kenny Green takes the stand as a character witness. Good old Kenny. He lived two doors down from my grandparents, and he is about ten years younger than me. I met him one day while cutting my grandparents' lawn. He's a good kid and a sports nut just like me. He always did like us Johnson brothers. He worked tirelessly to try to get me into a drug program. He's like my little advocate.

"Karl's a really great guy when he's not using," he says from the witness stand.

I'm feeling pretty good. My lawyer tells me that it wouldn't take this long if they were leaning toward a guilty verdict.

We are back in the courtroom. I'm nervous, but still feeling pretty good after the eight days of deliberation.

It's verdict day.

Judge asks me to stand and asks the jury if they have come to a verdict.

A woman stands, but I can't hear what she is saying because my heart is beating in my ears.

She is saying a lot of words, but all I hear is "guilty."

I feel like I'm going to faint.

I should have taken the three years.

Chapter Fifteen

If you meet the Buddha in the lane,
feed him the ball.
—Phil Jackson

Too much time goes by between my conviction and sentencing day.

There's a lot of drama in LA County Jail. There's a race war going on. The blacks and the Mexicans have to be separated on the buses because there is always fighting.

It's my day of sentencing.

They lead me downstairs to the holding cells before loading the buses and hand me number four.

I see nothing but Mexicans in the number-four cell.

"I'm not going in that cell."

No good things will happen if I'm in that cell.

"You are going in that cell."

I am not going in that cell.

I stand there showing as much defiance as is allowed in LA County Jail. I win for the moment, and they put me in a single cell. I would have been killed if I went in that cell.

Time to get loaded in the bus, but they put me in the cage with all the other prisoners. The Mexicans are spitting at me, and there is nothing I can do.

We finally get to Southgate Court in Norwalk, and I'm unloaded from the bus. I know I'm not supposed to be here for my sentencing.

Maybe I'm getting interviewed for the drug program.

My hopes are shot down when they load me back on the bus, after realizing that they brought me to the wrong court. No one says sorry for the humiliation I had to endure from the Mexicans on that bus to the wrong court.

Now it's September 11, 2001, and I'm headed back to court to be sentenced. Hopefully, the right court now.

But I never make it to court. I'm loaded on that black bus, but it doesn't move for three hours. We are stuck in the parking lot. Something is wrong.

The Twin Towers have been attacked in New York, but we don't know this. All we know is that we are sitting on the bus and going nowhere.

Finally, another guard comes onto the bus.

"New York has been attacked. Everyone's court date is cancelled."

There is fear that LA is going to be next. But I'm not scared of a terrorist attack. I'm just scared about how many years I'm going to be locked up.

There's gotta be a law that's been broken—I should have been sentenced two months ago.

The unthinkable terrorist attack on America is lost on me. All I care about is how much time I have to spend in prison.

I finally get to court for my sentencing on September 30, 2001.

"Mr. Johnson. Do you have anything to say?"

"Your honor, I really need a program."

"You get rehabilitated in prison."

There's no rehab in prison. I'm headed to level four security. It's about survival. Surviving has nothing to do with healing.

The total prison time I'm looking at is seventeen years because of my "priors." The total sentence is five years plus the seventeen years of priors. I am dealt a twenty-two year sentence.

I was prison hardened, but not prison hardened for what I was fixing to get into.

There are two guards on either side of me, walking me out of court. I'm light-headed and my knees give way, and I start to buckle to the floor. The guards grab my arms tight and help me up. It feels like I am being dragged away.

I look back to see Charlie sitting there. He's just looking at me with these sad eyes.

Just help me out where you can.

Even Charlie—who helped save our younger brothers and sisters from the house fire years ago and taught us all to swim—couldn't save me now.

I'm put into the holding tank. The Mexicans are in one holding tank with the whites, and the blacks and Asians are in the other holding tank. They always put the blacks and Asians together.

There are about fifty of us in that holding tank.

"What did you get?"

"Man, they just destroyed my life. I got twenty-two years."

"Hey, well I just got eighty," a voice over my left shoulder yells. "I'll take that twenty-two—let's trade."

The guys in the tank start trading sentences. Most of these guys are sentenced to life.

I guess it can always be worse. It still doesn't make me feel any better.

There are more whites in prison than people think. With this whole explosion of meth—there are a lot of whites in prison now. That wasn't the case for many years, though. The whites used to be messed over pretty bad in prison because they were outnumbered by the Mexicans and blacks.

Not now. There are a lot of whites in prison now.

I don't have a problem with anybody, and I certainly don't try to mess over people. My thing is that I can talk you into—or out of—anything. I can convince anybody that what I am doing is correct.

It's called the gift of gab—it served me well and will continue to serve me well in prison.

I'm waiting on the chain for about another forty days in LA County Jail before I catch the chain to state.

Kenny Green is the only visitor I have during that forty days of waiting on the chain. He comes and gives me thirty dollars. He's just a good dude. The thirty dollars will carry me through reception. I know I'm going to need that thirty dollars in state prison. I have to have some cash—a little insurance for survival in level four security.

Mama doesn't have a lot of money to give, and Dennis is done giving me money. In fact, my whole family is done with me. I feel alone.

My reception is at Delano State Prison. I'm scared to death. The thought of being locked down for twenty-three hours a day is freaking me out. They are having a hard time placing me. I'm at the highest security level, but I'm not violent.

They don't have problems placing violent offenders—they put them in the 180-designs. Two cells with a slab of concrete down the middle. Those who are less violent go in the 270-designs with no cement slab—not sure why they call it 270-design, because that doesn't make any sense.

Because this is a high-security facility, there are less 270-designs.

Reception is really hard. We get to go out into the yard just once a week. I am thrilled to breathe fresh air and feel the sun on my skin. But it almost isn't worth it because something is always happening in the yard. Someone is settling some debt to someone else.

I follow the program and keep clear of any trouble.

You have to always be doing something in prison to steer clear of the trouble. I keep myself busy writing letters. I'm not getting any response except from Mama and Kenny Green, so I feel kind of deserted.

I need money because I need to buy some shaving gear, and I want to buy a TV because I'm going to be in here a long time.

I talk to Mama twice a month and Dennis once a month.

We work out all the time in prison, lifting weights. My arms are so huge, and it's so uncomfortable, carrying around these big, bulky arms. It is hard to sleep with all this bulk, but that's what you do in prison.

My work-out partner is Shorty. He is only five foot ten inches tall and has shorter arms, so he is able to bulk up faster than me because he has shorter levers. My arms are longer, and I have more muscle to build. Shorty is smaller than me, but actually stronger than me.

There are the "shot-callers" in prison. These are the guys who literally control everything and call the shots at prison. Each racial group is called a "car." The black car shot-callers will call a shot against the Hispanic car. I steer clear of this, but I'm part of the black car. My skin dictates this. I'm not a gang member, so I can't hide behind that. I have no power—the guards are telling me what to do, the black car is telling me what to do. I don't want any trouble, so I do it. And I'm powerless.

I used to think I was so good at what I did, being one of the best runners of cocaine in Compton. I'm thinking now about how I could have been so caught up in that evil world.

I was a great salesman, but I should have sold cars or something legal.

Kenny Green continues to write me and send me some money. He gives me updates on my girl. Becky traded testimony in my trial for three years in prison. I'm not upset at her. I understand this game.

She didn't take her case to court, so she gets a deal. I understand now that I should have taken what they were offering me. When you use the court's money to go to trial, you are going to pay big.

I write letters to Becky and send them to Mama. She takes them out of the envelope and puts them into a new envelope and sends them to Becky in prison. This is how Becky and I stay in contact, prison to prison. I know this manipulation of the system will not last long. It works for a while since the letters are coming from the outside.

It's Mama who puts a stop to it after about a year. She doesn't like my girl.

Mama has better things to do, like go play bingo.

Mama is a professional bingo player. She goes to watch her boys play basketball during the day and then plays bingo all night, playing at the big Baptist churches. One of her favorite places to play is Mary Star High School in San Pedro. That's where all the women gather. She likes to take bingo trips to Las Vegas on the turnarounds.

Mama tells me during one of our calls that Renee is taking her to bingo now. Her driving is getting bad because her vision is not good. She's side-swiping cars. Just like they did with Granddaddy, my siblings have to take Mama's car away. But nothing is going to get in the way of her bingo.

I lie on my bed and smile to myself thinking about the time Mama asked me to go to bingo with her.

She wants me to go play bingo with her. She has this big old bag of the ink-things. I guess you call them daubers.

"Come on now, Karl, you come with me and I'll give you half of what I win."

"How do you know you gonna win?"

Mama has this system. As long as she's winning, she goes. If she has a dry night, she takes a little break. She won three days ago, and she knows she is due for another win.

"You just got home. You looking good, so let's go to bingo."

"I don't want to go to bingo, Mama. Just give me twenty bucks."

I go tripping in the neighborhood with her twenty bucks and she goes to bingo without me. She wins a thousand dollars.

Damn it!

"You coulda had half of this, but you wanted twenty dollars."

She's taunting me with all the cash in her hands.

"I'm going again tonight—you wanna go?"

No, I don't. I'm mad I lost out on that money.

Mama tried everything to get me off those streets. My heart feels a little heavy, as I lie here staring up at the cement ceiling. I guess this is the heaviness of regret.

I don't like to lie around. I read a lot of books and magazines. But I don't grow or expand my mind. I can't. I'm in prison. In eleven years, there's a lot that you can do in your life. You can expand your career. But I'm not doing anything but trying to look busy. Everything stops in prison. You have to figure out where you fit in all this madness. I am black, so I have to fit in with the blacks. It's a means of survival and staying alive. The Southern Mexicans are known enemies of blacks in prison. We just don't get along.

You would think the higher levels of security were the most dangerous. I start out in level four because of the length of my sentence, and I have sixty-four points. Three points for each of my twenty-two year sentence, minus the two points for my good behavior in LA County Jail. Level four is for anyone with thirty-eight points or more. There are no riots in level four. The problems start in level three, but I'm doing so good and I don't want to get mixed up in all this crazy stuff. There are four riots in just one year. It is chaos. Thousands of young black guys with like thirty-five-to-life sentences. They have nowhere to go, and they just don't care. They want to fight the Correctional Officers. They can't get any more time, so they just want to jump on the

COs—even if they kill the COs, they can't get any more time. And that's how these young black guys think.

My chin is gray, so I'm able to stay away from all that. Age is my protector, and I'm considered an old man being in my forties. Gray is respected in prison. And it's all about how you walk. I don't walk with the gang.

I wasn't a gang member on the streets, so I'm not part of the gang in prison. If you don't start right away in a gang soon after you arrive in prison, you're not going to be in one. I avoided the gang thing on the streets, so why start now?

I'm not interested in making my way here in prison. I've got plans to get to fire camp. I have been there before—it is only reserved for level one and level two security. I start training for fire camp three years into my sentence.

I don't get out of my cell very often while in level three security because of all the riots. There's always something going on out on the yard that can ruin your day. I know I need to get in shape for fire camp, so I improvise. I start doing "burpies" in my cell—drop down for a push-up with my legs spread apart, then jump back up and repeat. This is a great workout—works my arms, legs, and stomach. I also use the toilet to do step-ups to build up my legs. Up, up, down, down. I commit two hours a day to this because I know my legs are my weakest part.

I only do these exercises when my cellie is at his job because I don't want to annoy him. Most of these guys are lifers—they don't want to see me working out. I don't want to be fat and ugly like them. And I need to get ready for fire camp. I've got places to go.

Inmates bring me stuff because they want to own me. But I have enough homeboys to give me money and whatever stuff I need.

Friendships are different here in prison than on the streets. In prison, friends are a necessity for survival. They give you credibility and the cover you need. Prison friends are not like the friends I have on the streets. I never walk out in the yard alone because if a riot breaks out, I need my friends to protect me and watch my back.

I'm in my sixth year of my sentence, and now I'm in Centinela State Prison. I'm working on getting to fire camp, so I keep a strict program. I just try to stay out of trouble. I go to church every Sunday. It's my saving grace. I get into the vocational program and love learning new things because I can't stand not growing. Prison is a wasteland. Being in this vocational program for carpentry gives me purpose and keeps me focused. I get to go to class and learn a trade. I finish the program and get my carpentry certificate with a focus on dry-wall finishing.

I'm part of the LA area "car." Prison has this tribal thing going on. It's like we are all Indians, and we have our own tribes. I suppose it's the only way to make any sense out of the chaos. Interesting, though, that the inmates organize themselves like that. I guess it's no different than a bunch of kids playing on the playground, organizing themselves into groups.

There are the Bloods, the Crips, the Northern Mexicans, the Southern Mexicans, the Northern Whites, the Southern Whites, the Northern Blacks, and the Southern Blacks. There's an Asian car and even an Islander car. Then there are the Pisas—they are direct from Mexico. And a whole host of other races.

Any of these groups go off on each other at any time, so I have to stay with my group.

I have an inmate number that starts with a "D." These are some of the original numbers issued in the 1980s. I first get my D number in 1988, and it stays with me all these years. I'm D77034. It's a number I will never forget. If you have a "D" number, you know the program and you get respect with this kind of number. The COs know that I know the program.

Centinela is the worst place to be. The Southsiders are in control here. It's just chaos. I'm involved in several riots during my stay—not my doing, but just trying to protect myself. These guys are animals. At least out on the streets, there were rules. But we are locked up together and literally at each other's throats.

I keep up my workouts where I can, but I'm not feeling too good. It starts with this burning in my throat. I report it to the guards, and they put in a medical request for me. It takes a long time to get to the prison doctor. I finally get to see him a couple months later. He thinks I have acid reflux and puts me on Prilosec. The burning doesn't seem to be getting any better, but I don't complain because I don't want to miss any of my classes to get my dry-wall certificate. I'm on the Prilosec for about a year, but the burning in my throat continues.

Now I'm starting to lose my voice. I'll be in the middle of talking to someone and my lips are moving, but no sound comes out. My voice just disappears. I'm certain there's something else going on, so I put in another medical request. Three months later, I go back to the doctor. He sends me to an outside hospital, where they put a camera down through my nose. Sure enough, there's a mass the size of a quarter wrapped around my voice cord. I'm scheduled for surgery to get it removed.

Another several months go by before I get to surgery. I'm transported in a state vehicle with two guards. Cuffed in the backseat, I'm looking out the window, wondering where we are headed. I just do what I'm told. I'm nervous, though. I don't have anyone looking out for me. I'm really nervous to go under for the surgery.

I see a sign for Sea World. We are in San Diego. I'm thinking we are getting close, but the driver pulls into a parking lot in front of a bright green and yellow building. This is not the hospital. He gets out of the car, and the other guard stays in the car.

What is going on?

The guard comes out holding two paper-wrapped packages.

Unbelievable. They stopped for lunch.

All I can hear is something about jerk tuna.

Don't mind me, dudes. I'm just in the backseat headed to major surgery.

We finally get to the hospital, and I'm led to a hospital room by the two guards. I'm told to get undressed and get into the gown. They cuff me to the bed. I get an IV, and now I'm really scared.

What if I don't wake up? God, if you are listening, I'm sorry for all that I have done. I promise to do better. Just please let me wake up.

My bed is being wheeled down the hall to surgery. That's the last I remember.

"Mr. Johnson, do you know where you are?"

I open my eyes and see a nurse standing over me.

"What is the last thing you remember?"

Praying that God is not so mad at me that he doesn't allow me to wake up.

I'm just glad to be alive. And the news is good—the mass they removed from my vocal cord is benign. I get milkshakes and ice cream. This is a treat, but it is uncomfortable to swallow. My throat is really sore.

Less than a day after surgery, I'm back in prison. Apparently, they didn't get my prescription for milkshakes and ice cream. Back to the chaos of Centinela, but I'm happy to be alive.

On my tier, the blacks only have three of the thirteen cells. I'm working hard to shave off my points, so I can get to Sierra Conservation Camp in Jamestown, California—my last hurdle before fire camp. It's hard to stay away from all this rioting, though. If I get caught in this mess, points will be added, and it will be longer still before I can get to Jamestown.

There are six of us blacks on our tier headed to chow. We have to stay together, so we line up to go to the kitchen. We are on controlled feeding today—like we are most of the time because of all the fighting between the blacks and the Mexicans. The black shot-callers and the Mexican shot-callers have deemed it OK to walk to chow.

The guards are all lined up in the hallway from our cells to the kitchen. I can just feel the tension.

This is not good.

I'm not worried about getting hurt. I'm in the best shape of my life. I've been training all these years for fire camp. I'm worried about getting caught up in whatever is going to go down. I'm not in control here. The shot-callers and guards are.

I walk into the kitchen, and there are about five blacks already sitting and eating. It appears that the Mexicans have strategically placed open seats throughout the kitchen to spread us out. I see three Mexicans and one black sitting at the table in front, and three Mexicans and one open seat in the back corner. We are outnumbered.

This is not going to turn out well.

I'm a veteran inmate. I know that I need to jump up and get my back to the wall once this thing goes down.

My boys and I are taking our time getting our food trays. I sit down and scoop my first bite of potato spuds. The spoon is not even to my mouth when the chaos erupts. It's quick. A group of Mexicans jump up and attack a black inmate to my right. On my left, the Mexicans are throwing punches. I get hit in the head with a plastic tray, as I fumble out of my seat to get my back against the wall.

There are arms, legs, objects flying. There are blades. My back is against the wall to protect me from the animals coming from behind. I'm kicking and punching three guys with my back against the wall.

I have to stay off the floor.

Number one rule in a riot: Stay off the floor. If you fall, you will be killed.

This is level three, and these guys are wannabe killers. The real killers are on level four. Wanna-be killers are worse than real killers. They are desperate to get to level four. This world is so warped.

I hear the explosion. It's like a firecracker, and I know what's coming next. The guards move fast, but not fast enough. My shirt is already ripped off, and I have no shoes.

Where did my shoes go?

The yelling stops and gives way to the choking sounds. The room is filled with tear gas. I'm coughing, and the gas brings me to the ground. I start scooting along the wall away from all the guys. I'm trying desperately to distance myself from this.

Once the guards gain control, they take us back to our cells for body checks, where we will be searched buck-naked. If I have any marks on me, I am going to the "hole."

I can't go to isolation. I'm so close to getting out of here. If I go to the hole, I'm delayed another three months.

I'm checking my body for marks. I have a few scratches. No blood. But I know it's enough to send me to the hole. Doesn't matter who started it. If you have a mark, you participated. You are guilty.

The choices in a riot are only two, and they are not good: participate to stay alive, but get thrown in isolation, or don't participate and die.

The CO gets to my cell, and I'm standing there naked.

"Man, you know I'm trying to work hard to get to fire camp."

This plea even sounds pathetic to me. I just can't stand it anymore. I need to get out of this mess.

"I don't want to hear any of that. Do you have any injuries?"

"No, sir, I don't."

Please don't make me turn around.

My back is all scraped up from leaning against the wall.

"Johnson, I just want to know one thing—do you have any injuries?"

Why is he not making me turn around?

"No, sir."

He backs out and closes the door.

Man, God is so good.

That year, I actually get to go to classification twice where my points are reduced. You are only supposed to get reclassified once a year, but they are happy with the program I am doing.

Finally, I shave enough points off and get to go to Sierra Conservation Camp in Jamestown, California. I can't wait to get out of this hell here in Centinela State Prison. I pack all my stuff up. I can't take my TV, though. It's too big. It's the green one that Mama sent to me. I try to give it to another inmate, but I know that it will go to the prison. It has my number on it. No transfer of goods.

I climb on the bus. I can't believe I'm getting out of here. I have been training for fire camp for six years now, and I'm one step closer. It takes three days to get to Jamestown.

Our first layover is Tehachapi State Prison, and it's like coming home. This is where I started my prison term six years earlier.

"Johnson! How are you doing?" one of the COs says.

The COs are great here, and they remember me. They like basketball, and they like me because of my brother. Dennis provided me the cover I needed in prison.

I see one of my favorite guards, Moreno. He is from New York City, but he doesn't like the New York Knicks. He likes the Boston Celtics, and he is such a good guy.

He was nice to me, I know, because of Dennis. I respect him for that—to be from New York City and like the Boston Celtics, you're in trouble. After he got to know me awhile, he came to me one day with a newspaper all rolled up.

"Hey, Johnson, read this."

Inside, there was a basketball card of Dennis. Moreno was that kind of guy. He collected cards and wanted me to have it. I know that he would have gotten into big trouble if anyone found out. I like this guy. I noticed him in the middle of all the riots. He would get in the middle to take charge. I know he hated to see us fight. That was the thing about Moreno—I could tell he wanted good things for us inmates.

"I'm headed to fire camp," I say all proud-like to Moreno.

"Good job, Johnson."

Moreno is good to me. He gives me shaving cream, razors, and deodorant, so I can clean up a bit.

I feel like I have come full circle. I have made it in a way. I have made it through the fire, but I'm headed literally into the fire in camp.

We are in the R-n-R section of the prison. Not rest and relaxation, but receiving and release. We sleep on the floor. The next day we head to Pleasant Valley State Prison for another layover, and finally, on the third day we make it to Sierra Conservation Camp in Jamestown.

I want to go to the level one yard, but I still have too many points—twenty-eight points. I have to have nineteen points or less to be on the level one yard. I get placed on level two. No sooner do I arrive than level two breaks out in a riot and goes into lockdown.

It's between the blacks and the Mexicans.

Again.

I'm losing my patience. My plan is completely out of my control. These idiots keep fighting like they don't have a care in the world. I get right in the middle of this stuff again.

I have absolutely nothing. No shaving equipment. No deodorant. I don't have a radio, and I had to give up my TV. It's like starting over. And I have to do it in level two. Still have some more proving of myself to do before I can get to fire camp.

Almost there. I won't give up.

No one's talking in my dorm. The Mexicans aren't talking to me. Obviously. The blacks aren't talking to me because they don't know if I'm legit. Here we go again. The Mexicans outnumber the blacks—again. The rest are white. Everyone thinks it's just a bunch of blacks and Mexicans in prison, but that's not true. There are a lot of whites. The white car is big because of meth. White guys are using meth on the streets, and they are now in control. Whites and Mexicans help each other out. The Asians help us blacks. The hatred between blacks and Mexicans is so deep that it doesn't even make sense.

It's three months later, and we finally come off lockdown. I go out to the yard and walk the track.

"Quick! Quick! Quick Karl!"

I look up and see five of my boys from San Pedro.

"Man, we thought you had a life sentence."

"Yeah, everyone's been telling us you got life."

"Well, obviously, I didn't because here I am."

We haven't seen each other for more than seven years, since the year I did in LA County Jail waiting on my case before going to prison.

"I'm on my way to fire camp."

I say it so they know I'm no-nonsense. I'm not going to get myself caught up in any situations. They came straight from the streets and have been here for a couple of years. We head over to the basketball courts. I'm dying to pick up a ball, but didn't want to go there without a crew.

This is where I meet my best friend, Hot Link. His name is Johnny. He's a shot-caller and at six foot three inches and two hundred twenty pounds, Hot Link has quite a following.

We are out on the yard, playing basketball. I end up on his team. No one really wanted me on their team because I'm "O.G."—the old guy. With gray on my chin, no one's thinking I have anything to offer on the court. I don't know who Hot Link is other than a shot-caller. He's got these big calves—I call them rugby calves.

"That's DJ Johnson's brother over there," I hear someone say.

"Where you from, O.G.?" Hot Link asks, as we walk over to the bleachers after knocking off six games.

"I'm from Pedro. I'm Dennis's brother."

"Dennis who?"

"Dennis Johnson."

"I've been looking for you. Someone says you were on the yard. I didn't know it was you."

We sit down on the bleachers, and our connection is immediate. He's a Laker fan. We just start talking basketball. He's going on and on like he's some kind of sportscaster. He's a basketball nut just like me.

We play basketball every time we go out into the yard. We sit for hours in the bleachers, too, just talking basketball. It's like there is no one else around. I know I have a friend.

Hot Link is bald-headed, just a few years younger than me, and he's from South Central LA. He has a lot of pressure being a shot-caller, and he needs someone to talk to.

For years, I listened more than I shared. But it's different with Hot Link. I can share things with him. He's my friend, and we trust each other. You can't cry in prison and risk other inmates seeing you, but he can sit with me and cry. I would never give up anything he tells me. I sit with him, and soon the tears flow freely for us both. It's a weird kind of safety thing that I have not felt with anyone before.

As a shot-caller, Hot Link is always in the middle of stuff. Inmates are coming to him for advice and direction. He has to call the shots.

"Johnny, leave that stuff alone. Do something for yourself," I tell him.

"I can't, Karl. Once a shot-caller, always a shot-caller. People depend on me."

I can't help but think about Dennis. Lots of people depend on Dennis. When he was on the court, his teammates depended on him—the franchise depended on him. Off the court, he had a lot of family depending on him—his own family, his in-laws, and the Johnson family, including me.

It's tough to be the guy on top.

"Let those idiots be idiots," I tell Johnny.

Today, he's really down. There's a lot on his mind. There's too much that he's trying to control, and everyone is expecting him to control it.

He's listening to me. I have some kind of credibility with Johnny. I'm like Hot Link's advisor. I believe it's for no other reason than the fact that my brother is Dennis Johnson. Hot Link respects me for that, and I have an influence in these matters.

"Come on, man, let's hit the track."

We walk and talk. He tells me all about the crap that's going on and how he has to run interference. It's not little stuff, though. In his position, he has control over whether there is a riot or not, which can mean life or death.

"I'm in charge, Karl."

I get it. He has a responsibility to lead these idiots in prison. Sometimes it's personal, and he has to fight on behalf of his crew. It's part of the gig.

Stupid.

In general, there's a lot of fighting going on in the barbershop in the back corner of the prison. Inmates literally stand in line with the guy they are going to fight to wait for the guard to unlock the barbershop. Five guys go in, and five guys come out. There's Hot Link going in. I know what this means. He's in there refereeing the fight between two guys—it's the two fighters, Hot Link, and two other guys on watch.

The guards know what's going on. About thirty minutes later, I see Hot Link come out, and he heads over to me. The guards see these guys come out all ratted up with sunglasses on their faces. COs don't do a thing. It's part of the program here.

I work in the kitchen, starting at four in the morning. I get off at ten in the morning and stay behind to be searched out by the kitchen staff. I don't want to be searched out by the guards because they take everything you come out with, including the chicken and cookies. It's the one perk of working in the kitchen, and it gives me leverage. Cookies in the prison are like gold. If I make it out of the kitchen with a handful of chocolate chip cookies, I've got some good bartering to do. I get some good soup and deodorant. There are a lot of cookie monsters in prison.

The Southern Mexicans don't trade with me, though. They are not allowed to trade with blacks. The Mexicans are good people one-on-one. There's something larger at work that no one can control. This deep-seated hatred between Mexicans and blacks just can't be explained, and it can't be fixed. The whites and the Asians can trade with me, but not the Mexicans. The Mexicans won't let this nontrading rule between blacks and Mexicans keep them from getting cookies. They just have the whites or Asians trade for them. There's always a way around things.

More than anything, I like to work and earn money. You don't have a whole lot of worth in prison, so it is important to me to do something. I make eight cents an hour, which comes out to about twelve dollars a month. It doesn't matter, though. I have a job. I have some worth. I don't like calling home all the time asking for money. The money is drying up anyway. Mama is on a fixed income, and Dennis is just sick of me asking for money.

Truth is—I'm tired of asking for money. Once I get to fire camp, I'll be making more money, so I really won't need to ask for money.

Chapter Sixteen

Basketball is like photography, if you don't focus,
all you have is the negative.
—Dan Frisby

Mama writes me all the time. She writes a lot about her health. She's not doing so good. If it's not her vision, it's her legs. Mama's having a hard time getting around. And she's having a hard time seeing, which makes it even harder for her to write to me. She tells me in one of her letters: "Karl, please write more clear. I can't make out some of your writing."

Today, I get a letter from Mama that makes me smile.

Hi Karl,
I just wanted to drop you a few lines to let you know I am thinking of you. We are all well here and hope you are well, too. You know, Karl, it is 5:30 in the morning and I am wide awake and you were on my mind! I was thinking back to when you were a little boy and remember you was about two years old and we lived in Wilmington on O Street. Well, I guess I had told you that you was the baby, but then I went to the hospital and came home with Renee and you were so upset about it. I think you cried for two days because we had told you that you were the baby and then brought another baby home! You would not cry in the house. You would go behind the garage and cry and my neighbors called me to ask what was wrong with you. Well, I was just thinking about you and that came to mind. Well, Karl, you know I

will never give up on you because I know you are a good person and a good son, so I will keep on trying and praying to God to turn things around and let me see you come home again.

Love you, Karl
Your Mom
Margaret Johnson

Baby. I always wanted to be the baby. Her letter, telling me about this reminds me of being diagnosed with a "baby attitude" in that attack therapy I did years ago. They told me I had a baby attitude and wanted me to put on a diaper and climb into a crib. I guess there's some truth to this. Babies are selfish. They have to be to survive. I have been very selfish. My years of thinking in prison have revealed a lot of harsh things about myself.

I wanted to feel special. It's hard to feel special when you have so many brothers and sisters fighting for attention. I guess I got attention—I just went about it the wrong way.

Mama is always there for me. She is my constant support—my link to the outside world. Her words give me comfort. Mama still believes in me. She's such a good person. She has worked so hard her entire life, raising our family and taking care of other families in the community. That's just what she did—she would drop off groceries to families who needed help. She knew who needed a little extra help through her work with social services. She would ask me, "Karl, you have any friends that need some extra food?"

She's a remarkable woman.

Three months go by, and I have not heard from Mama. My calls go unanswered. I have not received any letters from her. I know something is wrong.

"Johnson, you have a phone call from your sister. Go take it in the office."

This is not good.

I instantly know it's about Mama. Inmates don't take calls in the office unless it's bad news. I saw a young black kid come out of that office just six months ago, and he was crying. I saw him a little bit later walking the track. I was told that one of his parents died. I wanted to go up to him and say something to him. But because of the stupid tribal rules in prison, I couldn't approach him—not even to give him some support for his loss. He was a gang member, so his people took care of him.

I start crying when the guard hands me the phone. It's Renee.

"Karl, sit down."

Why do people always want you to sit down before bad news?

"Mama's been in the hospital for three weeks. She's not going to make it."

"Oh, no." I'm choking to hold back the tears.

"She has asked about you, telling us to make sure you are taken care of."

Renee says a bunch of other things, but I can't hear what she's saying. I hang up the phone and just sit there. My counselor is in there with me, but he doesn't say anything. My head is in my hands.

I feel so alone. Mama is everything to me. I'm so selfish. I knew Mama wasn't going to be here forever, but if I had just taken the plea bargain, I would have been out by now. And I would have been able to see Mama.

I'm a selfish baby.

The ache in my heart is just too much. We are still on lockdown, so all I can do is lie in my cell, waiting on the bad news, knowing I will never see or talk to Mama again. Here I am lying in this damn cell when I should be by Mama's side. She was a wonderful lady who stood by my side all these years—through all the bad stuff. I can't be there to hold her hand. I want so badly to tell her that I love her for the last time. This hurts so bad.

A week later, the guard tells me I have a phone call.

My mama died.

I don't want to hear it, but I take the phone again in that office. I'm crying before I hear Renee's voice.

"Karl, Mama passed away this morning."

I feel like I killed Mama. The guilt is too much for me. It has a choke hold on me. I put her through so much. I was supposed to be a good kid, but I wasn't. If only I had been a better person, Mama would still be alive.

The anger I feel toward myself overcomes my grief of losing Mama. I'm stuck in my cell because we are still on lockdown. I don't have access to my group. I'm desperate for some support. I just feel so damn alone.

I talk to Dennis on an emergency phone call I was offered by prison officials the day of Mama's funeral. The conversation is a little strange. Something is not right. Dennis doesn't sound like himself. He's saying some odd things, and there is something eerie about the call. He's saying something about money, but I'm not listening. I'm talking. I do that a lot—just talk over people. It's because I have a lot to say, and I want details about Mama's funeral.

Now, more than ever, I want to get to fire camp. I'm determined to do what I need to do and shave off enough points so I can get out of here. I'm not sure I can do this without Mama's regular letters and phone calls. I am losing patience waiting for my "gate pass" that you get when you pass the physical tests for fire camp.

Less than a year later, I'm lying in my bed in the prison dorm when I see my brother's face flash on the TV. I walk over, but by the time I get to the TV, his face is gone. I ask the inmates what that was about, but no one caught it. Then fifteen minutes later, a guard calls my name, telling me prison counselors need to see me. My heart sinks.

The voice on the other end tells me that my brother, Dennis, had a heart attack and died today.

This is more than I can take. I break down. The counselor asks if I'm going to be OK, and I say yes because I do not want to go into isolation. I am still grieving the loss of my mother. The only way to grieve is to walk and cry on the track, but you can't let anyone see you.

"You need to go for a walk, Johnson?"

This CO knows me and is good to me. I walk and just keep walking. A group of my guys form a circle around me, so I can walk and cry. The pain is unbearable. Not only am I in prison, but my grief is also in prison, and that track is the only permissible place for tears.

My mind is racing, going back to that last phone call. The conversation haunts me. Something was wrong. He was talking about money. He seemed so stressed.

I never understood that the pressure he was under could kill him. Thoughts about all the times I asked Dennis for money, for shoes, for whatever flood my mind.

What was wrong with me?

My heart aches thinking about what an idiot I was. Just because my brother was DJ Johnson, I thought that the world owed me.

Then I start thinking about how he will never have the joy of being inducted into the Basketball Hall of Fame. His name has been on the list for years. I remember asking him about the Hall of Fame.

"It doesn't matter. It will happen if it happens. It doesn't define my career."

"But Dennis, it is defining your career."

I need to know more about my brother's death. I just don't believe that it was a heart attack. I try to get my hands on as many magazines and newspapers as I can to try to figure this out.

What went wrong?

I read this article in *Men's Health* magazine, "The Fit Man's Heart Threat." It talks about why so many athletes collapse and die from heart attacks.

There's not enough money in the world that is worth my brother's life.

I'm back in my cell now after walking the track, and my mind again goes back to our last phone conversation. He was talking about problems with money. At the time, I thought that was ridiculous because he had made millions of dollars. His voice didn't sound right. But I wasn't paying any attention. I was focused on my own needs.

I wish I had told him I loved him.

I don't want this feeling again. I will tell my family I love them every time I see them when I get out of prison.

I just wanted Dennis to be OK with me. I wanted him to know that I am a good guy. Now he never will.

Chapter Seventeen

Good, better, best. Never let it rest. Until your good is better and your better is best.
—Tim Duncan

I finally get clearance to go to fire camp—eight years into my sentence. My twenty-two year sentence was reduced to twenty-one and I am serving only half of that for good behavior. I'm making good progress, and only have three years left. I have made it out of those prison walls, earning points I need to go from level four security to minimum security. I will serve out my final years in fire camp, fighting fire.

I'm still raw from losing Dennis. Mama and Dennis were the only ones who called me in prison, and now they are gone. I'm further isolated at fire camp. I'm working in Fenner Canyon Fire Camp, and it is brutal. We are cutting seventeen miles of fire line a day, carrying heavy backpacks that feel like they weigh sixty pounds. This is hard work. I haven't worked this hard in my life—it's just backbreaking work. I remember working with Daddy laying brick. That was hard work, but we didn't work twenty-four hours a day. I'm up to about 225 pounds. I'm uncomfortable, but we have to load up on carbs to keep us going. I just packed on the weight. I'm now in my fifties, and this is a whole new ball game. And I'm sober.

What did I get myself into?

I'm not complaining, though. This is a privilege, and I do not want to leave. Just as in any situation I'm in, I figure out a way to be the best, earning the respect of the fire captains. I work my way up to second in command.

When fire breaks, there is no stopping until we cut the entire line. Cutting fire line is critical in stopping the fire from spreading. It takes a lot of tools and skill to cut the fire lines. The saw is the first on the line and cuts a path through the brush, and then the axe comes in and cuts the brush down to just a few inches. This axe is called a Pulaski, named after a forest ranger who invented this tool that is an axe and a hoe all in one. Pulaskis are used to cut the thick roots and clear rocks. Then there's the McLeod, named after another ranger. It's a six-pointed rake with a wide flat hoe. The McLeod is the last tool on the line and cleans up all the brush down to dirt—it's a fierce tool. All of these tools require special training to use, and we practice every day. The goal is to get the brush down to clean dirt to kill the fire. The line needs to be wide enough to stop the embers from jumping the line and becoming fuel again.

I am the drag spoon—the last guy up the mountain, who makes sure my crew and all their stuff gets up that mountain. I had to work my way up to this position by doing all the other jobs—I did Pulaski and McLeod work. We walk for miles, and I have the shovel. It's my job to make sure all the debris is clear from all this raking, hoeing, and cutting. Sometimes I have to go back down the mountain to get stuff that some idiot has dropped along the way. We climb for miles, and it's steep. It's so steep that when someone drops his canteen up ahead, I have to catch it before it rolls back down the mountain.

We are hiking in San Luis Obispo County. I don't like it here because the ground is really soft—makes it hard to get your footing. You take one step forward and slip two steps back. It's tricky, and you have to know where to step. If you step on a rock and it comes loose, you're falling. Our camps are in the mountains, and there are hikes you can take to practice. I practice every day because I know that this is serious business.

I hear yelling up ahead. I look up and see one of my crew members tumbling down the hill. He doesn't release his sixty-pound backpack, so that fuels his descent so it's even faster. He does let go of his tool, which he probably shouldn't have—he could have used that to grab into the ground and stop himself. He's going so fast and trying to grab tree stumps along the way. I'm reminded of the nursery rhyme "Jack and Jill." Except it's not Jill tumbling down, it's Willie.

Willie's just yelling like crazy, but I get out of his way. Willie's too big to stop. He's going to bowl me over. Once Willie starts rolling, he knocks everything down in his way. But not me because I just get out of the way. As the drag spoon, I've seen guys tumble a lot. Willie's new, and just like a lot of these new guys, he actually doesn't know how to hike—even though we have all endured the training.

He should have listened up during the hiking instruction.

In fact, our training was rigorous. It's ordinarily six weeks of physical training, but I did it in one week because I had five years of preparing for it while in prison. Before we got to go to fire camp, we had to pass the physical tests and the written tests. You have to run the mile in less than nine minutes, thirty seconds, and do other physical tests like hang on a pull-up bar and do harbor steps. I was in my late forties when I passed the physical test, and there were guys in their young twenties who could barely run the mile in less than thirteen minutes. It's because all they had done was sit around smoking weed.

Once you pass the physical test, then you get a gate pass, so you can go to the classroom and prepare for the six written tests that you have to pass. We watched a lot of videos about fire safety. I took a lot of notes. I passed the six tests. Then I went on to the three hikes that I needed to do in a certain time. I passed. This is not for everybody. Fighting fire is dangerous.

My name was put on the list to be called to fire camp. But if the blacks and Southern Mexicans got into another fight, then we all were on lockdown. Two months I was waiting to be called up, watching the white guys get called. It was so frustrating. I was not in control.

Finally

My name was called.

"Which camp do you want, Johnson?"

"Sacramento," I said because I knew I had to do reverse psychology.

I knew from experience that if you wanted to go south, you had to say north. It's all tactical because they know if you want to go somewhere, then you probably have a hook-up. I knew how to play this game.

Sure enough. I got Southern California—Palmdale. I was hopeful I'd see some of my family. If I just got close enough to LA, maybe I could see them.

I got to the fire camp in Palmdale, and I was calling phone numbers that no longer worked. None of my brothers and sisters had land lines anymore. Just cell phones. Calling a cell phone from fire camp required that you have money on an account, which I didn't have. The twenty dollars Mama sent a month stopped when she died. I had no way of letting my family know where I was except to continue to write them—letters that went unanswered.

I gave up on that. I was mad.

Why don't they write me?

Why don't they come see me?

Why don't they send me money?

Now, as the drag spoon, I call shots. I don't like calling shots on people. I was not a shot-caller in prison because I didn't want the hassle. But out here, you do what the captains want you to do, so you can stay. There are some perks to the job, too. Not only do I get paid thirty cents more an hour than the other crew members, I am taken care of in other ways. When cigarettes were eliminated, one of the captains brought in tobacco for me. They can get fired for this, but I appreciate it. We have each other's back.

We have to stash the tobacco on the bus. We are in such close contact with the public that every time we come back to base camp on the bus, we have to be searched. Sometimes the tobacco is found. This close contact with the public allows some inmates to get cell phones and even drugs.

We are fighting a fire up in Humboldt County, and the weed is literally on fire. Here we are a bunch of inmates, cutting fire line through a thicket of marijuana plants. I don't touch any of it—I'm here to do a job. Three inmates get caught stuffing the weed in their suits.

Stupid.

They get sent back to prison. They even face new charges and more time added to their sentences for drug possession and transporting. I don't want to go back, so I stay on the straight and narrow.

Temptations are all around. These guys are like kids in a candy store. I don't know what their problem is. You mess up, you go back. They don't care, but I do. There are huge risks in putting a bunch of criminals out in the public to cut fire lines. This is dangerous work, and we are expendable.

Just about a year after fighting fires in Humboldt County, we are down in the Azusa Mountains trying to protect some homes. There is one house that catches on fire. The flames just eat up this house. Our crew heads in to help the frontline firefighters, and the ceiling collapses. My crew is in the backyard now, and we are just watching this ceiling cave in and a big safe fall from the attic to the ground floor.

The flames are put out by the water and all that is left is black burning wood and smoke. And the safe that breaks open. There's jewelry and money all over the place. It's a chaotic scene, and the fire personnel are busy doing their job. I see about five of my crew members head over to that safe.

I can't believe they're doing that.

I don't yell out, though. I don't want to have anything to do with this, so I head over to the rest of the crew and help out with the hoses. People talk, and word gets to the captain that some of the inmates took stuff from the broken safe. Department of Corrections is called.

We are back on the bus, getting ready to leave.

"Everyone off the bus," our captain says.

All sixteen of us crew members climb out of the bus, and line up on the street as we are told.

"I'm going to give you a chance to come clean."

It's silent.

Damn it.

I know that the strip search is coming.

Just 'fess up.

I'm pissed. This is so humiliating. We are in the middle of the street in the middle of the day, and now we have to get buck-naked. The neighborhood has been evacuated, and it's just fire personnel and now correctional officers. It doesn't matter, though. I'm sick of this. I'm working so hard, and now I have to take all my clothes off and be searched.

Three officers search each of us at a time. They find money in shoes, in backpacks, and in canteens. One of the crew members was thinking ahead, and he "hooped" some of the money. The bending over took care of that, and he was discovered. In all, seven of them took some money.

Unbelievable. I just want to go home.

Now half my crew is gone. We are taken off the call list because we don't have sixteen crew members. An order for more inmate firefighters is sent, but it can take weeks until we are back up to our required sixteen crew members.

I can't wait to get back out there. There's a sense of freedom and purpose that I crave. The worst part of prison life was the lack of purpose, lack of movement, lack of growth. Finally, after just a few weeks, we have a full crew again and are put back on the call list.

It doesn't take long before we are called for duty. We are back in our orange Nomex suits, and we head out to cut fire lines again. The backbreaking routine starts again, cutting miles and miles of fire lines by day. Danger is real every day. Our Nomex suits protect us from the heat, but not fire. If we come into contact with fire, we will burn. We have to move fast. Fire will creep along uphill, but will turn into a wildfire before you know it. Where there is smoke, there is fire. I know this to be true.

Today, we are on a fire in the San Bernardino Mountains. We are on direct attack, which I hate. I have one foot in the fire, and I'm breathing a lot of smoke. My crew is uphill on the grade, and there is another crew down in the saddle, cutting line. I hear a bunch of yelling, but I can't understand the words.

I move downhill a few yards, and now I can see what is happening. The crew down in the saddle is being attacked by fire, created by a crew uphill who had set some backfires—a result of miscommunication among the captains. The crew in the saddle is caught in the middle. This is not good. My heart is beating in my throat.

No.

I'm frozen by fear, as I watch the Dolmar—the guy with a portable gasoline tank on his back for the chainsaw—run away from the flames. It's chaos. There's lots of yelling and running. Two inmate firefighters run past me, and I can smell the burnt skin. I remember this smell from when I was shot—it's a smell you never forget. We are helping the wounded inmates to the buses, where the ambulances will arrive to take them to the burn center. Luckily, no one was killed.

This danger is real. You can actually smell the danger. People are down there living their lives and these inmates are up here in fire camp, with one foot in the fire burn and one foot out of the fire burn.

Quiet comes at night, though. There is something so great about that quiet. In prison, there is no quiet. The clanging, clinking, chatter—never stops. But out here, there's real quiet. The darkness when night falls only lingers for a short time until the sky lights up with stars. Tonight, we camp under the stars. We find a place to sleep in the cow pasture—we never sleep on the mountain. I lay out my sleeping bag, hoping I'm not right on top of the cow shit.

Tonight, I'm lying on the ground, looking up at the sky. There are just so many stars. I breathe in the cool night air, listening to the sounds of creatures coo and screech. So many nights I lay in my prison bed, listening to the hollow banging and clanging of prison doors and the chatter of men in captivity. Not tonight. I spent most of my life doped up, not even noticing the stars. At first, not having the dope to help me cope with my prison life was almost unbearable. But by now, I have come to I like having a clear head.

The clarity of my thoughts scares me.

What am I going to do when I get out? Where am I going to go? Where will I live? Get a job?

Mama is dead, and her house is no longer my safe place.

My release date is within reach. But my fear of not being able to make it out in the real world overshadows my anticipation of freedom. I get up to go take a leak by the big oak trees. The tree must be a million years old with its knotty, gnarly branches. I look up, and there sitting on a branch is a furry animal with big old eyes.

It's an owl.

I have never seen a real owl before. I saw many owls in Mama's house, though, because she collected owls. She liked owls and had them everywhere—owl paintings, owl figurines, owl coffee mugs. I don't know much about owls except that they are said to be wise.

I look up at the wise, old owl. He looks around quickly—his head jerking in all directions. It's like he can see the world all at once.

That's it.

I realize now that Mama was owl-like. She saw everything. And she was wise.

I do my business and head back to my sleeping spot. As I return to the warmth of the sleeping bag, I notice an equally warm feeling inside my chest. It's a feeling of comfort and security that I have not felt for a long time. My owl encounter has left me with a sense that it is all going to be OK. Mama was here.

It is a privilege to do this work, but it's hard. My body hurts. I'm starting to feel like my fifties are slowing me down. I start asking one of the guards if he can find me an in-camp job.

"Can you find me an in-camp job?"

"Where you want to work, Johnson?"

"The laundry. I can do a good job in there."

The laundry is the job to have. You can make a lot of goods in there if you play it right—do a good job and you can get the perks.

"I'll see what I can do."

After two years working on the line, I'm moved off the fire crew to an in-camp job. I'm in charge of the laundry, and I run a tight ship. I do exactly what the guards want me to do. That's the thing with rules—you give a little, and they will take a lot. This is where I get to see Hot Link all the time now. I got to fire camp about four months before Hot Link. We couldn't believe our luck that we ended up in the same fire camp. We didn't get to see much of each other, though, because we were on different crews. With me being in the laundry now, we get to see more of each other.

The laundry room operates on specific hours. There are times to drop off and pick up. Each inmate firefighter has a box with his number on it. I know everyone's number. I wash and fold their Nomex suits, their shirts, pants, socks, and boxer shorts. Each piece of clothing has a firefighter's number on it. I wash the clothing, hang it to dry, then fold it and put in the right box. And I do a good job. I want everybody to look good and to look neat. It's a lot of clothes. There are 120 inmates, so that's at least one shirt, underwear, and pants for 120 inmates a day.

Some inmates like to play games, telling me that they didn't get their pants back. They do this because they want a brand-new pair of pants. They can't fool me. I know everyone's number and what I wash, dry, and fold every day. If it's in the laundry in the morning, it's all ready to go by the end of the day

"Johnson! What did you do with my pants?" Rodriquez says.

"Dude, you're number sixty-seven. I folded your pants and they are in there."

"Nah, man, they're not in there."

"Don't be messing with me. I folded number sixty-seven. I tell you—they're in there!"

Who you trying to mess with?

I have rules, and some of the firefighters don't like it that I have this control. I know what Rodriguez is doing. He wants a new pair of pants for a visit he's got coming up. I can't give him a new pair of pants, though. If I did that, there wouldn't be any pants for the new guys coming in.

We have like five new guys coming every week. This is good news because that means there are five guys getting parole every week. This kind of progress is not lost on me. I feel like I'm part of the system, helping guys get their clothes—all neat and clean—before it's time for them to get out. It reminds me that my time is coming soon. In nine months—the length of a pregnancy.

What am I going to do?

I'm nervous about getting out. Instead of having a baby, I am the baby. I have to learn how to walk, talk, and survive in the real world.

Some of the inmates come back from cutting line and go to the gym to work out. We have a beautiful indoor gym on base camp with wood floors and glass backboards. When they do this, they miss their time to pick up their clean clothes. There are rules, and one of the rules is that the doors open at three and everyone has an hour to pick up their clothes. If you aren't there by four o'clock, you don't get your clothes that day. The other rule that I enforce big time is no stashing of anything in the laundry. Inmates get sent back to prison if they get caught with tobacco or a cell phone, so they want to stash it in the laundry.

No way. I'm not doing anything to mess this up. I'm too close.

One evening several months after I started, I'm closing up the laundry about six o'clock. I've been here since ten in the morning, and I'm ready to go. I'm turning off the lights when I hear banging on the door.

"Johnson! I'm here to get my stuff!"

I go over to the door and open the top half of the door. I see Rodriguez standing there.

Unbelievable. Troublemaker is back.

"Laundry's closed. Come back tomorrow."

"What do you mean it's closed?You're standing right there. My shit is right there!"

"Sorry, man, you know the rules. You gotta pick up your clothes by four. You missed it."

I shut the door, and I know he's pissed.

Too bad. Follow the damn rules.

Hot Link comes up to me at chow and tells me a group of Mexicans came to let him know that they don't like how I'm running the laundry. They want me out, and they want Hot Link to handle it.

"I don't know what you did to them, but they are gunning for you."

"Well, they are going to have to drag me out of there."

"Rodriguez told me to have you removed or there's going to be a riot."

"Let those fools riot, then. I'm not going anywhere."

I can't go back to hiking. I worked two years in fire camp to get this job, and no one is going to force me out.

It's a good thing that Hot Link is my friend. I don't know what he did, but he handled it. I never heard from Rodriguez or his crew again. That's the thing with Hot Link—he's going to man-up every time. I reciprocate and make sure Hot Link gets to hang out with me in the laundry room. Johnny Hot Link gets good stuff, too. Whenever we get a new shipment of clothes, I put Johnny Hot Link's aside. Johnny Hot Link doesn't stand in any line. He and I always have new shirts to wear. It's just the way it is.

Rodriguez got caught drinking gin. They piss-tested him, and he was gone. No more problems after that. Everyone knows I run a good laundry.

Hot Link and I have everything we need in the laundry—a little refrigerator, a radio, and a TV. No one bothers me because they know I'm doing my job. I apply my strict rules across the board, except for with Hot Link, of course.

Here's Hot Link and me, watching our basketball and folding laundry. It's here that we can talk. And not just about basketball. Sometimes there are tears on our laundry. That's the thing with having the time to think and a true friend to talk to. Regret crawls up and bites you in the butt.

Dennis finally gets inducted into the Hall of Fame on August 13, 2010. I can't be there. My release date isn't until October 1—less than two months to go.

I don't even get to see it on TV.

Chapter Eighteen

Sometimes a player's greatest challenge is coming to grips with his role on the team.
—Scottie Pippen

After nearly eleven years in prison, I am released on Friday, October 1, 2010. I am out of court at 11:30 a.m., but I do not get released until 5:30 p.m.

I'm free. There's Charlie with his wife, Gwen, and my little sister, Renee, too. I'm so happy to see them.

All I want is a greasy hamburger. But there is a little technicality—a little old business—that I have to attend to.

There's an old warrant out for my arrest in LA County for a probation violation. Apparently, new technology was developed while I was in prison that matched me up to an alias I used—Joe Dotson. Not sure why I ever picked that name, but I sure am sorry to Joe for any trouble I may have caused him.

I spend my first weekend of freedom back in LA County Jail. I'm sweating it. I don't want to be here. I was told that I could get another two years for this probation violation.

On Monday, October 4, I'm back in the tank, and I'm the last guy there until they take me into court.

"I don't have any paperwork for him," says the judge. "What's your name?"

"Karl Johnson," I say.

Or should I say Joe Dotson?

That would have been kind of funny if I hadn't just served over a decade in state prison only to have the threat of returning to jail hanging over my head.

One of the public defenders stands up.

"I'm representing Mr. Johnson, Your Honor."

He explains that I was just released from state prison, having served eleven years for a twenty-two-year sentence and that there is an outstanding warrant for my arrest for a probation violation in 1971.

I can tell the judge is tired. I'm the last guy of the day. What I can't tell is if that's irritation written on his face because his time is being wasted or if he is truly frustrated with me for all of my shortcomings in the eyes of the court.

He looks over his glasses at me.

"I think you have served your time. It's time to go home."

Music to my ears. All I want is that greasy cheeseburger. They give me a property-release paper with Joe Dotson's name on it. I even have to sign it as Joe Dotson. What a joke.

Joe Dotson's not even a real person. He doesn't have any property. This is stupid.

Renee is there to take me home. I quickly realize that Renee has taken on the role of Mama. She was always Mama's right hand, helping with the house and all the babies. Renee and I have always been close—there's only eleven months between us, and we went all through school together.

Renee's tough. She left home right at eighteen years old. Followed Dennis up to Seattle and went to beauty school—she owned her own salon at twenty years old, then met her husband-to-be, Dennis, the cop. He's from south Philly, and Renee was just gone. She was done taking care of kids and wanted to have her own life. Eventually she came back to LA, though. She only has one child, but Renee's house is the hub—she takes care of everyone.

Renee takes me to Charlie's house. They have all this food for me. There's fish and that greasy cheeseburger I wanted. It tastes so good. Food always tastes better around Charlie, though. He's a good man. He's been married to Gwen for forty-two years. They have two kids who are all grown up now, and they are doing really well.

"How you doing, Karl?" Charlie says.

"I'm doing good now that I'm out."

"It's good to see you, Karl. You look good."

That's the thing with Charlie. He doesn't start telling me what to do. He just wants to know how I am because he wants me to be OK. I feel welcomed here—no questions asked, just acceptance. I think that this is how I would have felt coming home to Mama's house. Unconditionally loved.

"You can come here anytime, Karl. You are welcome here."

But this is when I am told where I will be staying. I feel like such a baby. My family is in charge, telling me where I'm going to live. I'm going to live with Renee.

What choice do I have?

Renee takes me back to her house in Southern California. I'm going to stay with her. Since she's taken Mama's role, she takes care of everyone, and that includes me. But her husband doesn't like me. I can feel the judgment. That's the thing with law enforcement—it's black or white. There's no in-between.

I am nervous about seeing my brothers and sisters. I don't feel connected to them. They didn't call and didn't write. All my letters went unanswered.

Renee puts me in her son's room. My nephew is off to college, so he's not there. I don't feel comfortable in his room. All his trophies and his stuff surround me. This is so foreign to me. I'm lying in this bed that's in a totally different world, and the feeling of panic comes over me. I can't sleep.

What am I going to do?

More than anything, I feel a loss of home. Mama and Dennis are gone. They were my home. I feel like I am lost forever.

Renee's house has a finished garage with carpeting and a TV. That's also where the washer and dryer are.

"Hey, Renee, you OK with me sleeping out there?" I say to her the next morning in the kitchen.

"Are you sure, Karl? There's no bed out there."

"Yeah, I think it will work just fine."

I just don't feel comfortable staying in the house with them. The garage has things that feel familiar to me, like a weight set. I can use the equipment like I did in prison. And Mama's stuff is in here—boxes and boxes of her pictures, paperwork, and her collectibles. I want to be by her stuff, which is now Renee's stuff.

I miss you, Mama.

Renee heads off to work. I know that the first thing I want to do on my first full day out of prison is to go visit Mama and Dennis at their resting place. My uncle's girlfriend, Kim, gives me a ride to Green Hills Memorial Park in Rancho Palos Verdes. It's a beautiful place, overlooking the Pacific Ocean.

This place is familiar because it's where Daddy is buried, too. I know that Mama is buried close to Daddy, so I head there first. Then I see her name on a headstone: "Johnson." The headstone is simple. Mama was simple, but a simply great woman. I drop to my knees and hang my head.

"Mama, I miss you. I'm so sorry."

I expected tears, but they don't come. The ache in my chest deflates my lungs.

I don't deserve to breathe.

It's like I'm heavy and nothing at the same time. I am certain this is the feeling of regret and guilt.

I killed Mama.

If I had just been a little bit better.

I put her through so much.

I don't know where Dennis is buried, so I have to go back to the information center to ask. He is buried up the hill a bit. When I come upon his grave, I can't believe what I'm seeing.

Dennis Wayne Johnson.

The headstone is just as simple as Mama's.

What is this? They couldn't do any better than this?

Dennis was the man. He was the world to me. Larger than life, and he's reduced to this simple headstone that looks like all the others.

I'm so mad and distracted by this insult of a headstone. He deserved the nicest headstone. I have a hard time finding the words.

"I'm sorry I let you down, bro."

Again, the tears don't come. I leave the cemetery feeling emptier than when I walked in.

Nothing makes sense. I have no routine. I have no car, and I don't belong anywhere. I'm homeless.

Gary comes around and has nothing but sarcastic remarks for me. He's bragging about having all this money—he does work hard at the Port. And he has always been smart, handling all the money. He's a mathematical genius. He gives me a pair of sunglasses as my coming-home present.

A pair of sunglasses—are you kidding me?

Here I am, fresh out of prison, trying to figure this all out, and he shows up with a pair of sunglasses. Maybe he forgot the time he came into the liquor store when I was working and asked for money. I gave him the entire thirty-six dollars in my pocket.

I feel nothing but judgment all around me. My family is suspicious of me.

I feel like they're always wondering, *Is he high?*

This bothers me because I've sworn off drugs. It's like they don't know the real me. I'm a grown man, and I don't feel like I need to constantly answer to them. They are over there drinking Cognac and getting wasted, but I'm the one who is being judged. I give respect, and I just want respect back.

It takes me four days to go through all of Mama's pictures and stuff. In the boxes, I find her owl collection. Mama loved owls. There are owl paintings, owl mugs, owl plates, owl figurines—everything owl. I never thought to ask Mama why she loved owls so much. But after seeing that owl perched up in the tree when I was in fire camp, I understand.

There are big scrapbooks of all the newspaper clippings of Dennis and all us kids. Graduation announcements and school awards—she captured all the good things that her kids did.

What good things did I do? Did I do anything that made her proud?

I feel like I let her down. Then I come across the picture of me in the newspaper, playing basketball at LA Harbor College. It's my favorite picture. I was never a big offensive player, but a great defensive player. This newspaper shot is of me sliding across the floor going after the ball. And Mama kept it in her scrapbook.

It's like I'm flying.

I hope this picture of me made her proud.

There's a picture of her and Daddy when they first got married. She's so young and beautiful. There are mounds of pictures of her with her children, and she's just smiling away. There's one with her standing in front of her rose bushes at the house in Rancho Palos Verdes. In one of her letters to me while I was in prison, she talked about those roses and the time she spent taking care of them. That's what she did. She took care of people, and she loved to grow flowers. Mama had the touch, helping people and things blossom.

Why didn't I blossom?

Renee takes me back to Green Hills about a week later. She doesn't get out of the car, but she reaches into the backseat of the car and hands me some roses.

"These are Mama's roses."

I look down at the white and yellow roses. I'm confused by Renee's words.

"When she died, I dug up the rosebushes in her yard and replanted them in my yard."

What a neat thing to do, keeping a little bit of Mama alive.

I climb out of the car, but Renee doesn't follow. She's not getting out of the car. Tears are welling up in my eyes, as I head over to the now-familiar spot where Mama is buried. I'm not even a few feet from the car when I lose it. I try to catch my breath. When I get to Mama's headstone, I'm sobbing. I'm just a mess. This second visit is so much harder than the first.

"Hi, Mama. I'm just so sorry for all the trouble I caused... I wish I could take back all of it now. All the bad stuff I put you through."

I speak the words out loud. The words are coming out in short, muffled sounds, as I work through the tears. I'm trying to keep my voice down to be respectful, but I have to speak louder so the words can fight through the sobbing.

"You were such a good person. Thank you for all that you did for me. You didn't deserve all the stuff I put you through. I hope you forgive me, Mama. I'm not sure I can forgive myself. But I'm gonna make it up to you. You always said that one day I will get it. I'm gonna get it, Mama. I promise you."

Damn this is so hard. Lord, I need your help.

The finality of her loss is tearing me up. I lay the roses on her grave. I owe Mama so much, and I plan to repay her for by getting it right this time.

Renee tells me that Mama gathered everyone around her bed when she was dying. She told everyone that Karl is coming home.

"Make sure he gets off to a good start."

But I can't get off to a good start with a bunch of judgment and suspicion coming at me from all directions. I'm finally free, and I don't want to answer to anyone. I have this big gorilla on my back, and it's so heavy. I have so much to do. I don't have a car, and now I have to learn how to ride all these trains. Everything is so different. This is hard. I gotta figure out which way to go.

My friend Kenny is one of the first guys I go to see. He works at the Toberman Neighborhood Center in San Pedro, helping to steer kids away from drugs and crime. They do good work there. Kenny helps kids to make the right choices and to live the right life.

I want Kenny to see that I made it. I made it through all this nonsense. But, more than that, I want to know what happened to Becky. Kenny knows Becky, and he's my link to her.

I go to Toberman House a few times before I finally catch up with him.

He's put on a few pounds and his full head of hair is gone. He's bald, but he still looks like Kenny. He gives me some money.

"If you need anything, now, you just let me know."

"Do you know where Becky is?"

He says he doesn't know where she is, but I know that he's protecting me. He doesn't want me to go down that path again.

"Man, Karl, you look so good. You want to play some ball?"

"Yeah, I want to play some ball, but where's Becky?"

I have to see her. I spent a lot of years in prison getting OK with her. I think I'm over the hurt of her selling me out, and now I just want to see her.

He wants me to promise to come back to speak to the kids about my experience. I told him I will.

We stay in contact by phone. Kenny Green is my friend and has been for more than thirty years. He's a helper, always helping people. He has helped Becky.

I go out looking for her and start asking around. I finally get a number for her and I call her.

"Becky?"

"Yeah."

"It's Karl."

There's silence.

"I just got back, and I would really like to see you."

"Yeah. OK."

I'm thinking this is more difficult than it should be. She's acting like she's mad at me. I'm the one who should be mad. She threw me under the bus. I'm not holding that anger anymore, though. I had nearly eleven years to think about all of this and work through it. I just want to understand where her mind is at. We make arrangements to meet in Wilmington.

Don't go to Wilmington, Karl, you'll never come back.

I can hear Mama in my head. But I just got to see Becky.

I take a two-and-a-half-hour train ride from where I'm staying with Renee. I get there about twenty minutes early. I'm back in my old stomping grounds. I feel a rush of excitement—this is the place where I was somebody. I was a Johnson brother. I was a basketball star. I was a drug star. I was even King Drug Man. I had purpose there—my place was solidified. This is all that everyone wants—to be the top dog in their neighborhoods. And that's what I was.

But who am I now?

It turns out to be a waiting game. She doesn't show up. I wait for an hour. She's not coming. It takes me four hours to get back to Renee's house. I'm beating myself up all the way back.

This is not what you should be doing. You need to make the right decisions, Karl.

What a waste of time trying to reconnect with Becky. She has no respect for me. Put me in prison for nearly eleven years and doesn't give it a second thought.

This world doesn't make sense to me. I put up a good front.

I'm scared.

I fill out mountains of job applications. Everything is done online, and I don't know how to use a computer, so I have to have Renee's husband help me. He's busy and doesn't have any time, and I know he doesn't really want to be doing this. I didn't get to learn how to use a computer in prison because I was a high school graduate. You only got to go to school in prison if you were working on your high school diploma. So I didn't get to gain any computer skills.

I apply for lots of jobs. I'm thinking a job at Home Depot would be good. I could drive the forklift.

Have you ever been charged/convicted of a felony?

I had to mark, "yes," to this on every application. I do not get one call for an interview. I get responses over and over again that my services are not needed. I'm frustrated.

Renee feels bad for me and gives me a job at her hair salon. She pays me good, but I don't want to work in a salon. It's boring. I want some good hard work to do. Not just sitting around sweeping hair off the floor. Sometimes I show up, and sometimes I don't. I know that I am disappointing her and not being gracious for the job she gave me. Renee is such a good person. She takes care of everyone. She would work around the clock to earn extra money to help others out. Now I'm just feeling guilty. This is just not working out.

I don't know how to live in this world. There's only one thing I know how to do—where I fit in—but, I can't go there again. I know this. I have no identity. The person I was before I cannot reclaim.

I've been out of prison for several months now. So much has changed since I left. Renee helps me get a cell phone, but I don't know how to use it. When I went to prison for the eleven years, I had a beeper. Renee gets mad because I lose it—I left it on top of a payphone. Payphone makes sense to me—put money in and dial the number.

The world outside of the prison gates is unruly—so much violence going on around me. The overwhelming racial tension between blacks and Hispanics pulses in the streets, and the gang members are in control. At least in prison there were rules to play by. Out here—it's wide open.

I'm just black, and I am the enemy. I don't fit here. I need to get away from this violence because it will find me. I'm not going to stay here because when you are on parole and you get shot, you get the violation.

I am so scared. That bridge that I was supposed to cross with Dennis is not here.

Mama treated me perfect. Mama's not here. There was going to be good things on the other side of that bridge.

I'm stuck, and I have to get out. I have to get away from here. I don't want any help from my brothers and sisters. The kind of help I need they can't give me.

They think they are helping me by telling me what to do and when to do it. I just got out of prison after nearly eleven years of people telling me what to do and when to do it. When they say "jump" in prison, you do it. You have to earn the little things. And I did everything they told me to do to earn the points I needed. I'm tired of doing exactly what people want me to do. I want to be free. Free of the guilt, the regret, and this constant feeling of owing other people.

I have a real problem now with people telling me what to do. I don't want their help. I want to do this my way. I want to get to a place where no one can tell me what to do.

When I was in prison, Mama told me that I should see a psychiatrist.

Why do I need a psychiatrist? I'm lying here in prison. What kinds of problems do I have?

She knew. She knew that I would need some big help when I got out.

Although I am not prepared for this life outside of prison, I know what I want. And it's simple. I want a job. I want to pay my bills. I want a car to go places. But, most of all, I want to have the friends I want to have instead of drugs and prison choosing my friends for me. I need my freedom. Renee's husband takes me down to the Department of Motor Vehicles, so I can get my license.

Renee and her husband have three cars between them. She changes up what car she drives, and I'm over here riding trains all over LA getting lost. I offer Renee $1,000 that I earned while in fire camp for one of her cars, but they don't want me to have a car, saying something about needing to get insurance.

I'm fed up. I don't have any patience for this.

I have only been out of prison for a couple of months, but it is time for me to get on down the road.

I go to the Department of Human Assistance in Compton, right across the street from Compton Community College, to get a housing voucher. I just need a little help with a place to stay while I continue to look for work. I have about $1,000 in my pocket, but I need that to buy a car.

I get there right when it opens, but the line is already out the door. I find the end of the line.

"Man, what is this? This is crazy," I say more to myself, but the crusty guy in front of me turns around.

"They started lining up at four o'clock this morning," he says.

I stand in that line for hours, and we are not moving. I'm so frustrated, so I head back to Renee's garage with plans to go back at four the next morning.

This time, I'm there about four thirty a.m., and I'm the sixth guy in line. It's a sure thing that I'm getting a voucher.

I finally get inside and sit down with one of the counselors. After a few questions, she's handing me a voucher for a hotel room in Compton.

"Are you kidding me? Compton? I can't stay in Compton.

This place is a war zone. I've been gone for too long. I have no identity here. No street cred. I'll get eaten alive here.

"No, I'm not staying in Compton."

"Mr. Johnson, that's all I can offer you. The room in Compton is all we have."

I'm not going to Compton.

I'm a little worked up because I'm in survival mode. I know if they put me in Compton, I'll be dead.

"I want to talk to someone else in charge," I say, as if I have any authority.

Here I am asking for help. But this beggar is going to be a chooser because I'm not ready to die.

After creating a bit of a scene and getting firm with this lady, she goes to get her supervisor—a big brother in a jacket buttoned so tight over his belly that I think that button is going to fly across the room and knock me out.

After explaining that I am not going to Compton, I end up with a voucher to a room in Wilmington.

I know Wilmington. This is my hood, but I didn't leave here on good terms. I've got a lot of enemies here. The hotel they send me to is about a block away from the Junkyards.

Unbelievable.

I just got done doing eleven years for serving cocaine in this neighborhood, and they are sending me right back in the belly of the beast.

The hotel is filthy. It's full of Southsiders—Hispanics who don't want my kind around. I left my sister's half-million-dollar home for this piece of garbage.

This isn't good. But I can't very well go back and tell them I don't want to stay there after making such a fuss about Compton.

I've got a place to stay for thirty days. The room is small with a bed and a small nightstand. There are about twenty-five of us who have to share a bathroom down the hall. This place is so run-down, I'm not certain I want to get into the sheets of that bed. I suppose I have seen worse during my years of serving. I'm clear-headed now, and I'm seeing things differently. *How did I get myself back into the middle of this mess?*

The hatred I feel from these Southsiders is scary. No one has my back. There is no black car and lines of power to dictate the rules here like there was in prison. If I'm caught on the wrong street, I will get shot. This is a whole new ballgame.

Pacific Coast Highway divides this area and defines the battle lines of this cultural war. I know that I have to stay on the east side of PCH where the blacks are. The Hispanics stay on the west side. Blacks and Hispanics are enemies. It's just the way it is.

I don't have anything to do with this, though. I never gang-banged with these guys. I was a part of Compton when Compton was a step up. No one cares about the history of this place, though. The gangs own the neighborhood—and they own the history.

I get a few threats. I don't have a gun, and I can't have a gun. There is nothing good happening here. I make it twenty days. I have to get out of here. I don't want to go back to prison.

I leave all my stuff behind at the hotel because I can't take it with me on the streets. I would much rather live on the streets than with the threat of being killed by the Hispanics.

I'm walking the streets of LA with nowhere to go. At night, I'm sleeping next to a Dumpster in an alley. I'm just curled up next to it. This is a good place. Not a whole lot of activity.

At least I'm not sleeping in it.

I'm scared. The drugs are all around me. The pull of the drug is just too much, and I use cocaine for the first time in more than a decade.

It's like an old friend. I need the comfort. I just need to get out of my head.

Disappointment.

Guilt.

Regret.

Frustration.

Desperation.

It's just too much for me to handle.

I need help.

I end up going to a buddy's house in Compton. I hadn't seen him for years even before I went to prison. I just show up at his door.

It's about six o'clock in the evening. I knock on the door.

"Who is it?"

"It's Karl Johnson, man."

"What the hell?" He opens the door.

"Come on in."

We sit in the living room. He wants to know where I've been, offers me a beer. I take it. I'm gonna need it.

"Man, I just got out of prison serving about eleven years. And I just started using again."

My words hang in the air.

"Can you help me out?"

I feel like a complete failure. I never wanted anyone's help. I never needed it before.

I need it now.

He tells me about a friend who runs a halfway house—a sober living house. He makes a phone call and takes me into downtown LA to the halfway house.

I'm getting $221 a month from general relief. I can't get food stamps because I have been convicted of selling drugs. I go to the sober house in downtown LA and hand over my check for a place to stay.

The guy running the house is Ron. He's in recovery himself, and he remembers me from state prison.

"Hey, you're Dennis Johnson's brother!"

"Yeah, that's me. How you doing, Ron?"

Ron takes care of me. I don't have any money for cigarettes.

"Man, I got you."

Ron gives me cigarettes.

At first I think I'm in a safe place. But it is not safe. These people in here are nuts. Literally, they are mentally ill people. I don't belong here. They are all on medication. If they don't get their medication, they start throwing things at each other.

Unbelievable. I'm in a house full of crazy people. How is this helping me?

We only get one plate of food a day, and this is making things really tense. People get edgy when they are hungry.

One day I'm sitting there eating my plate of food and this black guy gets up from his chair with a fork in his hand and goes after Ron.

"I want food!" the crazy guy yells.

I can't do this. I'm falling apart. I'm going to end up back in prison.

I can't think clearly because I have these crazy idiots running around, attacking each other with forks over food.

I make it only about five weeks—clean the entire five weeks.

I should have stayed with Renee.

I end up at my baby sister Janett's house in Bellflower. She lives with two of her adult daughters.

She takes care of me, giving me money and a place to stay. I try to keep clean by keeping busy, doing yard work, and cleaning the house.

This isn't working. I feel myself slipping fast. And I know I need help, but I don't need the kind of help that my sisters and brothers want to give. This tough love stuff, telling me what to do, doesn't work for me. I have to get out of here. I'm teaching myself how to use the computer and the mouse thing. My niece shows me how to get on the Internet, and I search for the Salvation Army.

There's one in Eugene, Oregon. I think this will be a great place to be. Janett's oldest son, my nephew, lives up there, so I will have someone up there in case I need something.

I call the number and ask to talk to someone about coming up there and getting into their program. A guy named Rex gets on the phone, and he starts asking me all kinds of questions. I get the sense that he's not sure about me. Not sure about having a guy fresh out of prison coming to his program.

"I'll tell you what. You call me tomorrow at 6 a.m.," he says.

What? Six o'clock in the morning? What's up with this guy?

The next morning, Janett comes in and wakes me up.

"Get up now, Karl, and make that call."

There it is again. Telling me what to do.

I get up and call Rex.

"Hi, Rex, it's Karl. You told me to call you at six, and so I'm calling."

"Good morning. I want to talk to you about our expectations here. You have to be at least fifteen days sober to get into our program."

I got this.

"Yeah, I know. That's not a problem."

"That's good. We have strict rules here, so I want to be sure you are ready for this. I have to go now, so call me in three days at six a.m."

Three days later, I call him. We don't talk for very long. He seems distracted. He tells me to call him in two days again at six in the morning.

This is bullshit. This guy doesn't want me to come to his program.

Forget it.

I'm pissed, but I go back to the computer to look for other programs. I see that Fresno has a Salvation Army, so I call. The guy is real nice to me and says I only have to be sober for three days to get into the program. Not a problem.

Now I have a plan. I tell my family I'm headed to Fresno, so they all pitch in and give me some money. Janett throws me a party for my birthday—January 15; I was born on the same day as Martin Luther King Jr. Several of my brothers and Renee come to my party. We have lots of food and a nice cake. I feel good that they came to celebrate me. I have a few beers. It's so great to be with my family just having a good time.

When everyone leaves, I'm not ready to stop partying. I have a small rock of crack in my stuff, so I go out for a bit and smoke it all by myself. It's my birthday. I deserve this.

The next day, I get on the Greyhound bus headed to Fresno, but I have another plan in my head. I'm just going to keep on heading north to Seattle to look up Randi. We had such a good time together back when Dennis was playing for the Sonics. I have enough money to buy the ticket to Seattle once I get into Fresno.

I'm looking out the window, watching LA go by. I'm a little sad to be leaving my family, but I don't belong here anymore. I'm not sure what lies ahead, but I need to do this on my own. I have to get away from people telling me what to do. I just can't handle it.

The bus pulls into downtown Fresno on January 17, 2011. It's cold and overcast. Something has changed in my head during the bus ride. Suddenly, buying a ticket to Seattle to meet up with a girl I partied with more than thirty years ago doesn't make any sense. It did last night while I was smoking crack. Seattle was Dennis's town. He owned that town. He was big there, and I was big there because I was Dennis's little brother.

I walk around downtown Fresno. There's not much going on here. It's not a bustling place with lots of people. There is enough going on, though, and it's maybe the pace I need. I walk down Van Ness Boulevard with my rolling backpack, and I get this feeling that this is the place for me.

I head to the Salvation Army and ask for the counselor who I spoke with days earlier.

He comes out and shakes my hand. His name is Dan, and he remembers me.

"As I said on the phone, you need to be sober for three days and you need to test clean. We can test you today, and if you don't pass, we can't accept you into the program."

Well, I guess I won't be testing today. My birthday celebration is messing me up.

"Thanks. You know what? I will come back in a bit."

He asks if I have a place to go and tells me about the Fresno Rescue Mission, so I head out. I'm just walking around scouting out places. I arrive at the Rescue Mission too late. I didn't know that you had to be there by six to get a bed.

Shit. Don't panic, Karl, you got this.

I find a little cutout in a building along Van Ness Boulevard and curl up in front of this little coffee shop.

The next morning, I'm back walking the streets. I really need to find a job. I see three black guys tearing down a building, and they don't look like they are too enthusiastic to be doing it.

"Hey, can I talk to you a minute?" I yell to one of them through the chain link fence.

He walks over to me and looks irritated that I interrupted him.

"We don't have any work. What do you want?"

"I will work for thirty dollars a day. Come on, man, I need some work, and I can work circles around those guys."

He turns and looks back at his lame crew, then back at me. He's thinking about it.

"I'll give you twenty-five dollars a day. Come back tomorrow at nine o'clock."

OK. I have a job. Finally. Now I need a place to stay.

I head back to where all the homeless people camp out next to the Poverello House, a homeless center where us "poor people" can get a meal, actually take a shower, and wash our clothes. Salvation Army guy told me that's where I could go to get some food. I stand in line outside waiting to get in to get some food. There's this big black guy in front of me. He's talking to everyone and waving at people as they pass by. It's clear he has the respect of folks here.

I need to know him.

"Hey, man, I'm Karl," I say and stick out my hand to shake his.

"Hey, I'm Nate, but these fools call me Big Nate."

He's a big black dude and seems to know the scene really good. Has a bunch of tents in Tent City, he tells me. I still have my rolling suitcase with me, and explain that I need a place to store it while I go to my job tomorrow.

"I'll pay you five dollars to store it in your tent."

"Sure, man."

After lunch, I follow Big Nate back to his tent.

"You can have one of my tents. That one is mine, and that one is mine, and that one is mine," he says, pointing to three other tents placed throughout the site.

No wonder he has the respect—he owns lots of tents. I pick the one next to his. I don't know anyone here, and he is quickly earning my trust. Big Nate is an alcoholic. He says he graduated from Fresno State University. I have no reason not to believe him because he's smart.

The camp is just down the street from the Poverello House. Some of the people in the camp have a nice setup, using plywood and tarps for walls. People are people, and they are going to do what they need to do to survive.

My tent is raised up on a pallet with carpeting underneath to keep it up off the damp, cold ground. I climb into it with my suitcase and zip it up. It smells a little like wet dog inside, but I feel safe in here.

"G'night, Karl."

"G'night, Big Nate. Thanks, man."

We spent many nights in the dirt in a sleeping bag while we were fighting fires. So, the fact that I'm sleeping in a tent doesn't bother me. It's like I'm camping again in fire camp, except I don't have a sleeping bag—just my clothes to serve as my pillow and extra layers to keep me warm. January in Fresno is cold. It gets down into the thirties that night.

Damn it's cold here.

I wake up early. I remove one of my shirts that I wrapped around my face to keep my nose from getting cold and running.

I have to go to work.

I unzip the tent, and there's already a small crowd around the fire. The smell of campfire is so familiar that this feels like home.

Big Nate is standing by the fire, holding a Styrofoam cup of coffee.

"You want some coffee, Karl?"

"No. I gotta get going. Does anyone know what time it is?"

There are no clocks here. No cell phones to check the time. I'm just hoping someone has a watch.

"It's a quarter to eight," says a raspy female voice.

I can't quite see her because she's hidden by the campfire smoke. I yell out a "thank you" in her direction.

"Thanks, again, Nate."

I head out for my first day of work. I'm worried about my suitcase all day long. Everything I own is in it, which isn't a whole lot.

I feel good at the end of my first day.

God, it feels good to work.

"How'd, you do, Karl?" Big Nate says, as he gets the campfire going.

"Man, I can work circles around all those other fools."

"Got your stuff in my tent. Just wanted to keep my eye on it."

I'm so relieved. Big Nate's a good guy, and God is so good to me. I head to my tent early because I'm so tired from all my physical work today. More than that, I know I have to stay away from the bad stuff that lurks here. I need to stay clean, so I can get into the Salvation Army.

I lie down in my tent and wrap my clothes around me like blankets to shield me from the cold.

This is not so bad.

I start thinking about Mama and Dennis, but the shame that comes over me is too much for my tired bones. I push the thoughts out of my head.

This is no different than fire camp.

In the morning, I go back to work, tearing down this building. I work for three days, earning twenty-five dollars a day.

It's time for me to go back to the Salvation Army. I've been clean for four days now, and this is what I need to do. I have to get away from the darkness. There are some good, smart people living here in the homeless camp. But this is where I can see me slipping again. I have to get away from here—the drugs are everywhere. I was told in prison how hard it is out here. I never had a hard time getting a job before. I've been out of prison for a little more than three months, and I feel like I have gone backward. The easy thing to do is to succumb to this scene again. But, I'm an old guy now, and I haven't been on the streets hustling in over a decade. The street scene is the same, but the characters and the environment are different. I don't belong here.

I didn't belong in prison.

I didn't belong in my sisters' homes.

And I don't belong in a homeless camp.

I just can't go down this road anymore—I cannot go back to prison. I want to hustle clean.

It's my last night in the camp. I go down and get some hot links to cook on the fire and some chili. Big Nate and his friends have been good to me. I want to show my appreciation.

"Thanks for the chili dogs, Karl."

I have my hands deep in my pockets, trying to stay warm, as I smile.

"Whatcha smiling at?" It's the raspy female voice again.

I try to keep to myself. Don't want to get too close to anyone here. But I'm feeling hopeful tonight.

"Was just thinking about my brother. We used to go down to the swimming pool and buy chili dogs."

"Ha! I used to eat chili dogs with my family, too."

I think this is kind of a stupid thing to say. I'm sure everyone eats chili dogs with their family.

So, why am I in a homeless camp, eating chili dogs with all these characters? Not for long.

I climb into my tent for my last night. It's another cold, foggy January night in Fresno. Wet, damp fog came in early this evening. The warmth of the fire is quickly gone, but I learned the first night to bring my clothes to the fire to warm them up before climbing into my tent. They get fire smoke on them, but at least they carry some warmth. I wrap up my body in my clothes. The thought of sleeping inside in an actual bed tomorrow night at the Salvation Army fills me with hope.

The hope is replaced by disappointment, as I think about my family. The disappointment that I felt toward them for not helping me like I thought they should is now directed at me. This is an unfamiliar feeling for me. I used to think that it was never my fault—that people should have done more for me.

Karl, you better get on the ball. You gotta do something for yourself.

I suppose it is called humility. This homeless camp, sleeping on the ground in a tent, and using my clothes for blankets—this experience is opening my eyes. I have a choice—go back to drugs and the life I was living before prison or get my shit together and get the help that I need to get better.

Mama knew I would someday get it.

I think I finally got it. Humility.

CHAPTER NINETEEN

A tough day at the office is even tougher when your
OFFICE contains spectator seating.
—NIK POSA

NOW THAT I think I have learned humility, it's time for my salvation. I ask for Dan when I get to the Salvation Army.

"Welcome back, Mr. Johnson," Dan says.

Dan's a good guy. He's a former user. He went back to school and got his degree from Fresno State, and now he's the head counselor. And he's from the LA area. That is our connection—he's from Hawthorne; not far from San Pedro. Dan's the same age as me, and we know some of the same people.

This is where I'm supposed to be.

"If you don't test clean, it's going to cost you."

"I know, Mr. Dan, I'm good."

I piss clean. I'm in. I'm a little nervous because I'm just hoping that this program is not like that residential program Dennis found that I did years ago. That was attack therapy. I just need something straightforward.

I don't know anyone. They are all from Fresno. The building is three stories with really nice rooms. Of course, anything seems nice to me after camping out the last four nights. I have to hand over all my personal belongings. I get to go to the store and pick out my wardrobe—several pairs of jeans, shirts, shoes, and a couple of jackets.

Almost all of the people here are court-ordered. I'm not court-ordered and that's a good thing. I actually want to be here—I'm not told to be here.

I get to my assigned room with three other roommates. They are not in the room right now. I go down and take my first shower since showing up in Fresno. I get three meals a day and get to work. Most of us work in the store. I get assigned to the sorting department—picking out the good stuff from the bad stuff.

I like this.

Finally, I have some quiet time to gather myself. I have three meals a day, a bed to sleep in, and a job to go to. I'm just flying through the program. I'm focused on the program and following the rules, but I just spent nearly eleven years of my life being told what to do and when to do it. I'm starting to feel resentful.

You can't leave your work station.

You have to ask to do this.

You can't talk to your colleagues during work.

I start to feel suffocated by all the rules. Almost a hundred days out of prison, I'm being controlled again.

Salvation Army's drug program is formed around the Twelve-Step Program. I go to the classes that they tell me to go to. I just sit and listen to the others. I'm not comfortable getting up and proclaiming my addiction for several weeks. The others start to look at me with suspicion. I decide it's time for me to participate.

"My name is Karl, and I'm an addict."

I'm learning stuff that I already know. It's all about finding your "real" problems—the reason you started using drugs to begin with. I have to write down the names of people that I did wrong and write about what I did.

I'm just going through the motions. I've been through this before.

It's a lot of church—three nights a week in church. This is where we have all of our meetings, too. We start at seven in the morning sharp—you can't be thirty seconds late. There will be consequences if you are late.

We pray and go over the agenda for the day. Then we all go to work. We work until about three in the afternoon and get an hour before we have to go to our drug classes. I have three drug classes a night.

Did anything happen during the day that made you sad? Mad?

Did you feel like using drugs today? When? Why?

Do you feel anger toward anyone?

Did you feel like you wanted to hurt someone today?

This is getting exhausting. I have a chance to earn "night passes" permitting me to go to the store in the evening to get a cup of coffee. This is an earned privilege, so I can feel like I'm a normal person and "go out."

On the weekends, we walk to Cornerstone Church in Downtown Fresno for our Narcotics Anonymous meetings. I try to find someone from Fresno to walk with, so I can learn more about this town.

Every day feels the same. I feel like I'm in prison again. The routine is nice, but I want to feel normal, and I don't feel normal here. It's not that I feel like I'm better than all these people. I know I'm just like them.

The program is co-ed, but I'm not allowed to talk to my female colleagues. The only female I'm allowed to talk to is my supervisor, Rhonda. She's in charge of the clothing department. I find her looking at me every now and then. I want her attention, so I do extra jobs for her, wiping down the doors, sweeping the floors, anything to get her to notice me.

She eats alone in the lunchroom. All the supervisors are on one side of the room, and there she is just sitting alone. One day, I'm sweeping the floor in the cafeteria—to be helpful and to get her attention. I'm not supposed to talk to her until she speaks to me.

"Why do you eat alone?" I finally say to her.

She looks up at me and shrugs her shoulders. "I just like eating alone."

The door is open. I asked her a question, and she responded. I'm encouraged.

"Unbelievable. You don't want conversation?"

"No. I just want to eat alone."

Not taking the hint, I keep talking her up. I'm a talker. All this silence during work is driving me nuts. She gets up and goes back to work. I like her.

I have a few extra dollars from my monthly stipend, so I go and buy her a Snickers candy bar that night. The next day, I leave it on the table where she sits every day for lunch. I leave the room before she gets in there, so she won't know who left it there.

I do this several times, careful not to talk to her in front of others. I don't want to get into trouble. I don't think she knows it's me, leaving her candy bars.

I have worked really hard and have moved up from my position as sorter to janitor. I like this promotion because now I'm my own boss. I get to call the shots on what needs to be done.

I'm on my knees, painting the baseboards one day, as Rhonda comes walking through the door. She's all dressed up.

"Looking good today." I say to her.

"Oh, thank you," she says with a smile.

"Why you all dressed up today?"

"Oh, we're shooting a commercial for the Salvation Army, and I'm in it."

I really like her. It's been eleven years since I have been with a woman, and I've been out about a hundred days. I'm thinking this is a good sign.

She's pulling up in a car a couple days later with a guy. They both get out of the car and head in different directions.

"Who's that guy?" I ask as she comes through the door that I'm wiping down.

"That's David, my boyfriend. He works here, too."

"Well, how tight are you guys?"

I'm really trying to figure out if there is an entry point here. I like a good challenge, anyway.

A couple days later, I'm called into the office with the head guy. He's an ex-user and just intimidates everyone. If he says jump, we say, "how high?" He's articulate, antagonistic, and intimidating—three things together that just make me shiver.

Fraternizing.

I'm in trouble. He hands me a piece of paper that says I have been fraternizing with my supervisor.

Now I'm pissed. I worked really hard to earn awards and do extra work. I scrubbed floors, painted baseboards—I even painted all the bathroom walls. They don't give me any awards. Now I'm being called out for fraternizing with my supervisor.

"I need you to sign this."

"I'm not signing anything."

"Well, if you don't sign, you're out of the program."

Fine. I don't want to be here anymore. I'm sick of being told what to do. I feel like my entire life, I've been told what to do. My brothers told me what to do, the guys I served drugs with told me what to do, the prison guards told me what to do, and now the Salvation Army is telling me what to do. I'm just sick and tired of it.

I'm done. I've been clean the entire ninety days here. I got this.

"I'll tell you what—I'll make it easy for you. I'm out of here."

I'm escorted out of the door and allowed to go get my belongings that they took from me when I entered the program.

I'm free.

CHAPTER TWENTY

Be strong in body, clean in mind, lofty in ideals.
—JAMES NAISMITH

I'M FREE, BUT I have no place to go. I'm not going to call my family. They will think I am a failure.

I go back to the Poverello House to secure another tent. Thank God, Big Nate is still there. It's only ten thirty in the morning, and I need to head out to look for work. I leave my suitcase with Big Nate and start walking around downtown Fresno.

I go back to the guy who gave me the job demolishing the building before I started the Salvation Army program. He told me to come back to him after I got out of the Salvation Army. He's bartering again.

"Man, you got any work?"

"I got a few things. I can offer thirty dollars a day."

"No, man, that's not going to be enough."

Now my pride is getting in the way, but right is right.

"Well, then, I don't have any work for you."

More than pride—it is self-respect that makes me walk away.

I need a job to keep me busy.

I head back to camp to claim my tent.

"He's back again," the familiar raspy female voice says, as I walk down Big Nate Row.

It's late spring now, so the evening is warmer than when I left in winter. The warm spring evening brings temptation. The drug dealers are back with their wares. I don't judge—they are not bad people. I have to steer clear of this stuff, though.

I can't go back to prison.

I know my addiction will get the better of me if I don't stay busy. I can't just hang around the homeless camp, so the next morning, I head over to the Poverello House to take a shower and shave my face.

Shoe shining has always been in the back of my mind. I learned in prison that you can make a pretty penny shining shoes. And it was a big deal in prison. That was a cream job, getting the chance to shine the guards' shoes. I never got that job, but I did shine shoes for inmates. I had to be careful because you can get into trouble with the guards for shining shoes. I could not have a lot of shoes in my cell because the guards would find out. So, I would shine them out on the yard when we were playing dominoes. I was a popular person for shining shoes and would make a little money or get things like a can of tuna in payment.

When my brothers and I were little boys, Daddy would make us shine our shoes every Saturday night before Sunday church. He had been in the service, so he knew how to do it right. Daddy also shined shoes at the country club in Texarkana, so he knew the business.

Shoe shining is my back-up plan. I had been planning for it, so I have a rag and two polishes—one black and one brown. I have an old milk carton, too, that I found, so my customers can put their foot up on it. It's time to put that plan in action. I have no more options—living the bad life of drugs on the streets is not my path anymore. I owe it to Mama and to Dennis to do the right thing no matter how hard it is.

I'm going to beat this. And I will do it with hard work.

After my shower and shave, I head down to the courthouse because that's where the lawyers are. I sit outside in the courthouse park, trying to hustle a shine.

"Hey, your shoes need some shining!" I say to a bearded man in a gray suit, carrying a briefcase.

His shoes are all scuffed up.

"I'm late for court. I'll see you when I get out of court."

When that guy comes out of court, he heads in the other direction. I know he's avoiding me.

The first day I'm there, I get one guy to stop and get his shoes shined.

Every day, I get up to shower and shave at the Poverello House and head to the courthouse. I'm there by nine a.m. I'm not getting many shines.

"Your shoes are a mess. Just let me shine them." Now, I'm almost begging for someone to stop for a shine, sometimes even chasing them down.

This sucks.

I'm sitting there on the benches outside the courthouse with my cans of polish and a milk crate for my few customers to put their feet on. I know I'm looking kind of ratty. I'm clean-shaven, but my shoe-shine operation doesn't look so great.

I feel like giving up, but I don't have another plan. Mama wouldn't want me to give up, and Dennis never gave up all those years sitting on the basketball bench with no hope of real playing time. When things were looking really bleak, Dennis would just work harder, coming home from high school basketball games with only minutes of play time. He would go back out in the dark to shoot hoops. Then, after being told by Compton Community College that he was not good enough to play at the junior college level, he just worked harder. I'm thinking about all those recreation leagues that he played. He just kept at it, and that's where his break came when the coach of Harbor Community College saw him. The rest is history.

Just thinking about Dennis makes me feel a little better. If he can do it, so can I.

I just have to keep at it.

I look up, and here comes this nice-looking white man with blond hair and clear blue eyes. He's not running away from me. In fact, he's coming right to me.

I jump up.

"Hi, there. You ready for a shine?"

He smiles in agreement, and I go to work. My mouth is just running a mile a minute.

"What's going on with all you lawyers? I practically have to tackle you guys to stop. People need to know that you gotta take care of your shoes."

I'm going on and on. His name is Bob Whalen, and he has such a friendly face. He's a city councilman for the City of Clovis. He's easy to talk to, and he has a lot of interesting things to say. We talk politics. I know what I'm talking about because I pay attention. I read the newspaper.

When I'm done, even I am impressed with the shine.

He hands me fifteen dollars. I can't believe it. I made fifteen dollars with one shine.

I can do this. I can go somewhere with this shoeshine thing.

"Thanks, Bob. I appreciate you stopping."

"Thanks, Karl. Shoes are looking good."

"Hey, where do the lawyers go to lunch around here?"

"Most of them head to the Downtown Club on Kern Street."

"OK. I'll have to check that out."

I sit there every day until about two in the afternoon. That's when things really start to slow down at the courthouse.

The next day I'm ready to follow the lunch bunch when they exit the courthouse. Sure enough. It's just before noon, and there is a mass exit from the courthouse. I follow the group down the street, and a big group of them make a left onto Kern Street.

There it is—the Downtown Club. Bingo.

The brass sign with fancy writing reads: "The Downtown Club." The group goes in the door, and there's a small sign that says: "private club." I keep walking like I have some place to go. I do have a place to go now. I realize that I need to set up across the street, so I can grab them when they come out of the club.

What excuse can they use now? "I'm going to lunch?" I won't buy it now. I got them.

There is a small red-brick retaining wall that I sit on. I get out my polish and set down my crate, getting ready for action. There's a nice shade tree, and I'm right in front of the Fresno County Elections Office.

Lunchtime is a perfect time to get a shine. This plan feels good. The next day, I don't go to the courthouse. I go straight to that red-brick wall across from the Downtown Club. This is my new spot. I'm getting customers left and right. I made more than forty dollars a day the first three days I worked on Kern Street.

On the fourth day, it's about ten in the morning when this man comes out of the elections office. He's well dressed and his shoes are shining. I know that he has some sort of status. He's looking at me, checking me out, but he doesn't say anything.

I'm sitting there on the red-brick retaining wall, and I see lots of people stopping to talk to him.

Who is this guy?

I come back the following Monday because I'm keeping professional hours—Monday through Friday. There's no shoeshine action on the weekends, anyway.

It's only been a week, but I feel like I belong here. This is the spot where I am meant to shine shoes. Things are picking up a bit, and I'm starting to see familiar faces.

"How's it going out here?" The well-dressed man says.

"Well, you know, I'm doing OK. I'm Karl, by the way—you want a shine?"

"Nice to meet you, Karl. I'm Victor Salazar." He avoids my offer, as he does every time I offer.

"You coming back tomorrow?" he asks.

"Yes, I'm coming back tomorrow!"

He walks away. Just then a guy I've seen a couple of times walks by. I think he works in the same office as that Victor guy.

"Hey there! How you doing?"

The guy stops.

"Hey, who is that guy?" I point toward the door as Victor goes in.

"That's Victor Salazar."

"I know, but who is he?"

"He's the Fresno County Elections Officer."

"Oh. Thanks, man."

The next day, Victor comes out right around ten in the morning again.

"Hey, Victor!"

He comes over and hands me a nectarine.

"Thanks, man!"

"Looks like you doing pretty good here, huh?"

"Yeah, it's picking up. Once people get to know me, they know they are going to get a good shine."

"It takes time. I shined in Los Angeles when I was a kid."

"No way! I'm from LA—San Pedro."

"You coming back tomorrow?"

"Yes, I'm coming back tomorrow."

Just like clockwork, Victor comes out every day about ten in the morning, hands me a piece of fruit, and asks how it's going and if I'm coming back tomorrow.

"Are you coming back tomorrow?"

"Hell, yes, I'm coming back tomorrow!"

This little spot has become a hot place for me. I'm now a fixture. People know me, and I'm getting to know who is who and where they work. I'm getting lots of lawyers to stop now, as they come and go from the Downtown Club across the street.

My friends in the homeless camp know that I'm shining shoes downtown because they see me get up every day to shower and shave and leave for work. They are starting to call me "Shoeshine." I don't let anyone know, though, how good I am doing. Just like in prison, you don't want to show-off—it just brings unwanted attention. And any attention in the homeless camp is not positive.

I am disciplined—get to my spot every day by nine in the morning. I want my customers to know they can count on me being there, and, honestly, I need this routine. It just keeps me going. This street feels like home to me, and I'm hustling again—it's clean hustling, and it feels right.

I belong here.

Kern Street is my stage. People are yelling out to me from across the street: "Hey, Karl!"

I do my homework, too. I read the *Fresno Bee* every day—I have to keep up on current events because I need to be able to hold a conversation with all my customers. I'm interested in what's going on. I always read the newspaper in prison—didn't matter what it was. I was always reading stuff. People are just so damn interesting to me—I like to see what they are doing and why they are doing it. That's why setting up shop on the street is the best. I get to people watch all day long.

And talk about interesting. The local political scene in Fresno interests me. What's so different here in Fresno is that politics is accessible. The players are right here on my street. No sooner do I read an article about a certain city councilman than he's walking right by me. Los Angeles is just so big that no one really matters there. Here, in Fresno, I seem to matter. And I'm a politician of my own—I'm a street politician.

I like the feeling that I matter.

I've been out on Kern Street for about a month. People start leaving their shoes with me. I'm so amazed that they would trust me enough to leave their shoes behind. I like to think that I have good character and a good heart, but you never know what people are thinking about you. I just have to behave right, and they will think good things of me. This is when I start to see myself differently. People trust me, and they are coming to me for a service, and I don't let them down.

Victor comes out of his office one day, carrying a brand-new wooden shoeshine box.

"Here, Karl. I thought this would help you out."

He hands me the box, and I look down and see the Kiwi brand name on the box—this is a legitimate shoeshine box. I can't believe it.

"Man, Victor, this is amazing."

I'm blown away. I'm just staring down at the box, getting all excited because I will now look like the real deal. My personality and my street-hustling have gotten me this far, but this shoeshine box sends a message that I've got some credibility in the shoeshine industry.

"Thank you."

Victor doesn't hang around too long. I know that he doesn't want this to be awkward for me. There are a couple new shoe polishes in the box and a place for my customers to rest their feet. I don't have to use that dumb milk crate anymore. Victor's smart, too, because he also gives me this green foam kneepad, so I don't have to kneel right on the cement.

I'm shining shoes left and right. My little service is turning into a business. Mama never threw out shoes, and to this day, I never throw out shoes. I shine them to bring them back to their worth. You gotta take care of your shoes. They get you places. It's never too late to make something shine again.

I smile, thinking about Mama's words in one of her letters:

"I know you are a good person and a good son, so I will keep on trying and praying to God to turn things around and let me see you come home again."

I'm sad because I would love for Mama to see that things are turning around for me. And even though I'm technically homeless—I have found home.

That saying "it takes a village to raise a child" comes to mind, but in my case: it takes a village to keep a man straight.

That positive feeling that I got months ago when I got off the bus in downtown Fresno is turning out to be true. This town is giving me a second chance—the people here are helping me to live the life I am meant to live.

After Victor gives me the box and kneepad, I consider him my friend. He's a busy guy, too. He's always walking back and forth from the Downtown Club, and everyone knows him. My shoeshine spot is in perfect eyeshot of the club. I'm watching the new, shiny cars pull up, and I pay attention to who gets in and out. Local business leaders, politicians, lawyers, all kinds of people are just coming and going from there.

When Victor isn't busy having lunch at the club, he starts taking me to lunch. He takes me to a Mediterranean restaurant right there on Kern Street and introduces me to the owner, a short man with a friendly smile.

"You shining many shoes today?" the restaurant owner asks when he comes by.

"Not too many today."

"I got a little job for you, if you're interested."

"Of course I'm interested."

"I got a stack of flyers advertising my restaurant. If you hand them out to everyone who passes by, I'll give you twenty bucks."

"Twenty bucks? I wouldn't do it for thirty!"

He starts to walk away.

"No, man, I'm just messing with you. I'll do it."

Twenty bucks just for handing out flyers!

I love this. It gives me another purpose other than convincing people to get a shoeshine.

"Hey, there! There's a new restaurant over here. If you're not gonna get your shoes shined, then go over and try out this restaurant."

It's another hustling job—and I'm hustling clean. And it's sort of like economic development. I'm helping out this restaurant, which helps out the local economy. If he stays in business, he's able to provide jobs. I'm part of a community, and I have a role here.

This is good.

I can't wait to tell Victor about it. He is pleased that I picked up another job. I don't know if Victor knows that I am homeless. I don't mention it because it really doesn't matter. And he doesn't say anything about it.

Another guy comes by and wants me to pass out flyers for him. My name is getting out. Between shining shoes and passing out flyers, I make a couple hundred bucks this week.

This is good.

I can't lose here on Kern Street. I'm having lunch again with Victor at the Mediterranean restaurant, and I get up and start cleaning up and taking out the trash. The owner says he will give me ten bucks for cleaning up and emptying out the trash after he closes each day.

Just to empty the trash.

He lets me take all the leftovers from that day—he either gives it to me, or it goes in the trash. So, I'm taking like four containers of food back to camp each day and handing it out in the homeless camp. I give it away to the people who are hungry.

I'm giving back.

Of course, the business mind in me starts working. Even though it's a Mediterranean restaurant with kabobs, they also have cheeseburgers. I know cheeseburgers would be a popular item for the drug dealers—they are the ones with money.

So, I sell a few cheeseburgers to the dealers hanging out. I always take the hummus for myself. I have never had hummus before—I was missing out! I know what good hummus is about. It's all about garlic.

And it's good for my heart.

I'm eating good, though. My customers are bringing me lunch and asking me to lunch. Soon I have so many lunch dates that I'm all lunched out.

I've got a legitimate job. I'm feeling good. I'm not quite making enough money to sustain a living, but I'm not giving up. I don't want to do it, but I go down to the Department of Social Services to see about a little help. Anything I can do to keep on this path of "normal living," I will do.

I walk into the office with my backpack and wooden box. I want it known in here that I'm not some loser—I'm working, but I just need a little help. There is a male security guard standing in the waiting room with two female security guards.

He comes walking over to where I'm sitting and points to my box.

"Maybe I can get you to massage my feet, too."

The two female security officers start laughing.

They are laughing at me.

Now I'm just pissed. I mean I really thought I was something walking into this place with my box that said I'm willing to work for a living. These security guards are just laughing at me.

"Dude, you know what? I take offense to that."

They think this is even funnier. My blood is boiling. But what makes me even more pissed is the fact that one of the female security guards is black and she's laughing at me. She's quite a bit younger, so probably doesn't understand that you just don't do that—especially to your own race.

I get up and walk out. I can't stay here because it is going to get ugly. I leave before I can get my business taken care of.

About a week later, I go back down to take care of my business. That security guard is there.

I look at him as I walk through the door with my wooden shoeshine box. The look on his face tells me that he remembers me. I just walk right by and go sit down to wait for my appointment.

Here he comes.

"Hi, there, how's it going?"

I don't respond, but I do look him in the eye. That's the least I can do when someone is speaking to me.

"Look, man, sorry about what I said last week. I'll bring some shoes for you to shine."

"You know what, dude? I will never shine your shoes."

He doesn't know what to say. There is silence between us, but I'm still looking him in the eye. He knows he screwed up. That's the thing with people—you have to treat people good. That's what Mama always taught me. Don't matter what color your skin is or how skinny or fat you are. People are people. You have to treat them good.

But what really chaps my hide is that young black security guard thought this whole thing was funny. After all that we black people have gone through, she is going to stand there and join in on this ridicule of me. She doesn't understand the pain.

I suppose I get the last laugh—or at least a chance at the last laugh. I know God is testing me. Not a few months after all of this, I'm standing at my bus stop and look over to see a young girl outside her car that's pulled over on the side of the road. She's yelling something through the driver's side window.

Man, that's the female security guard that laughed at me.

It is clear that the guy in the car doesn't know what he's doing. He keeps on trying to start the car, and she's just yelling.

Part of me is just enjoying this scene. She's in trouble. Just seeing her conjures up that feeling of worthlessness. She played a role in my ridicule. And that still hurts.

Who's laughing now?

I walk over to her side of the car.

"What's the problem?"

"We ran out of gas."

I can tell she doesn't want to talk to me—clearly I don't have any gas on me, and she's thinking I'm of no use to her. It is also clear that she doesn't recognize me. After that incident of her laughing at me when I was being ridiculed, I would never forget her.

I get closer to the car as the dude inside continues to pump the accelerator.

"Dude, you got to just keep your foot down on the accelerator as you turn the key—don't flood the engine."

The pathetic whir turns to the rev of the engine. It starts.

"Thank you so much," she says.

"Hey, no problem."

As I walk back to the bus stop, I smile to myself. I had an opportunity to get the last laugh, but I didn't. Someone needed help, so I helped.

People are people.

I climb onto the bus and look out the window at the world going by. I'm thinking about all the times that I was so out of my mind, when I would have behaved like an idiot in this situation. I feel like I'm ten feet tall. Not because I helped someone, but because I didn't let someone else's behavior control mine.

I'm in control of me.

This is big. Mama said that one day I would get it. I just "got" part of it.

I see those security guards again when I go down to one of my appointments. I don't bring my box anymore, though. I don't know how they feel about their jobs, but I feel good about mine.

That's the thing about shining shoes—I want people to feel good about themselves. I don't care if you are dusty and dirty, you are a person, and you deserve to feel good. That's just how I am.

I know I'm on the right path, but I have to get out of the homeless camp.

Desperation lives here.

Evil lurks here.

People come by my tent, asking for like fifty cents. If I don't hand it over, they call me a bunch of names.

I'm the only one who gets up in the morning and goes to a job. They know I have money. Now I'm thinking it was a mistake to bring back food. I want to help other people out, but now I'm realizing that some people just can't be helped.

"Hey, Shoeshine, let me use your bike!"

This young man with a bit of a reputation who fulfills the drug needs of some of the campers wants to use my new bike. I just bought it because I'm sick of waiting on the bus. I just want to be in control of getting myself places, and this bike gets me to work.

"No, man, you can't use my bike."

"Dude, I need it. Just for tonight."

Not sure why I do it, but I let him take my bike. He doesn't come back until two days later. I'm pissed.

"Where's my bike, man?"

"The cops came and they was chasing me. I had to jump."

"Well, you need to pay me at least what I paid for the bike—twenty bucks, man."

"I'll give you fifteen."

I'm mad at myself for letting this fool have my bike. I know that he sold the bike. Now I'm back taking the bus every day until I can save up to get another bike. Several weeks later, I'm sitting at the bus stop, and I see one of his friends ride by on my bike.

There goes my bike!

"Hey, fool, that's my bike!"

The guy turns around to see that I'm chasing after him. He stops.

"Dude, that's my bike. You know that's my bike because I loaned it to your homeboy."

He gives me the bike back.

Nice.

These guys don't know who they are messing with. I've got years of street-living and hustling on them. I don't fight like I used to. I'm old now. I know how to get to the heart of an issue and work it out. I know one thing—I wasn't giving up on getting my bike back. That's my ticket to getting to my job every day.

Nothing is going to stand in the way of my job.

I encounter all kinds of interesting people on the streets. I don't judge them, but you gotta know how to handle them. You just gotta get into their head a bit. When they come up on you all crazy and aggressive, you gotta match that aggression and deflect it. You gotta talk fast and get them going in another direction.

Chapter Twenty-One

Things turn out best for the people who make
the best of the way things turn out.
—John Wooden

If I haven't said it before, I'll say it again: Fresno is stinking hot in the summer!

There's something about the heat that agitates people, too. What makes it worse is that it doesn't cool down, either, at night. That's the thing. It's like people are pissed that we endured all this heat during the day, and when nighttime comes, we want to be rewarded with some cool air. Not in Fresno in the summer. Sometimes it feels hotter when the sun goes down. It's as if the heat gives permission for crazy stuff to happen.

I know heat. When I was doing time in the Chuckawalla State Prison in Blythe, California, it was so hot that my skin turned purple. I remember being out in that yard, watching these lizards—they actually call them Chuckawalla Lizards. These lizards would be out there in the scorching sun doing these little push-ups on the rocks. I suppose it was their way to survive the heat.

Surviving the heat in a homeless camp takes some serious skill. Some of my fellow campers are just not right in the head. I'm not scared of them because I know how to handle them. Like Willie with his wild hair and even wilder eyes. He doesn't make a whole lot of sense most of the time.

I'm in my tent one night, and it feels like it's still ninety-five degrees out. It's about ten o'clock, and really it's only eighty-five degrees. I feel like getting buck-naked because it's so damn hot, but I can't do that here. I see my tent move.

"Shoeshine! Shoeshine!"

What the hell?

Whoever it is, they are trying to knock on my tent like I've got a damned door. I unzip it and see Willie.

"What's the moon doing, Shoeshine?"

Oh, boy.

Just two weeks ago, I found Willie at the bus stop with no clothes on. He does that sometimes. I can't say that I blame the guy, though. This Fresno heat is something else.

"What the hell you doing, Willie?"

"I'm telling you we need to get going. The moon is on its way out."

"The moon ain't going anywhere, Willie. This is what you gotta do. You gotta go over here now, and have a seat. We are going to get you something to eat. And you are going to be quiet."

I'm talking fast and loud. This is the thing—I'm talking loud and clear to get control. I grab a nectarine from my backpack, and I walk Willie over to his side of the camp.

He's rubbing his arms up and down like a madman.

"Willie, stop that."

"There's bugs, Shoeshine. Bugs all over my arms."

I distract him with the nectarine.

"You get in your tent and eat this nectarine."

"What about the moon, Shoeshine?"

"You don't pay any mind to that moon. The moon is out, so that means it's time for you to go to sleep. Now, you stay in here and go to sleep."

I walk back to my tent, thinking about what Mama and Dennis would think about this. It's normal to me. I don't want it to be normal for me anymore, though.

Dealing with all this crazy is normal, and it's not the worst thing—seeing a guy get killed when I was eleven was the worst thing. It's just time to get onto something different—I need a new normal.

I have got to get out of here.

Thank God I have Victor as my friend. He's like my lucky charm. Ever since I met him, good things have kept coming my way.

I know it's because Victor is so well-respected. He's a quiet man, but I know he's up to something.

A few days later, I find out that my hunch about Victor is right. A nicely dressed woman comes out of the Downtown Club and walks across the street. She looks familiar, and she's coming straight toward me.

"Hi. I'm Vanessa. I'm the manager of the Downtown Club."

She hands me her card.

"When you get a chance, can you call my secretary to set up a time for you and me to meet? I would like to talk to you about some work."

My heart does a little flip.

"OK. I'll do that."

She walks away. Now I really can't wait to tell Victor, but I know that he's behind all of this.

When he comes out of his building later that day, I ask him about it.

"No, I don't know anything about that, Karl."

Yeah, right.

I'm just so excited. I know that important things happen in that private club. I'm wondering about what kind of work they have for me. I don't waste any time in calling Ms. Vanessa.

I'm getting a little frustrated because her secretary is not giving me an appointment. It's not easy for me to find a phone to call from.

One of my shoeshine clients is a lawyer named Tim Cox. He's a family law attorney, always running back and forth to the courthouse. He lets me use the phone in his office. I call for three days straight, and I finally get Vanessa on the phone. She has time right now to meet, so I hang up and run across the street.

I hesitate, looking at those fancy letters spelling out "The Downtown Club." I have my backpack and my wooden box and no place to put them, so I walk right into that private club with my shoeshine box and backpack.

"I'm here to see Ms. Vanessa. I have an appointment."

There's just something empowering about having an appointment to see someone—it's like having a ticket. In here, it's more like a golden ticket.

"Your name, sir?"

"Karl Johnson."

Or should I say, "Shoeshine," like they call me in the homeless camp? Or "Quick?"

I smile to myself, shaking my head at the strange path my life has taken—from dealing cocaine in the Junkyards to being the laundry man in prison to shining shoes to standing here waiting to hear about this opportunity to work for a private club.

"I would like to add you to our menu of services to our members," Vanessa says.

I don't think I understand what she is saying.

"We would have you set up your shoeshine stand over here and offer your services as part of our member package."

I'm still not completely clear on what she's proposing.

"We would make it known that members would give you a donation or tip for your services."

I'm not sure about this, but it would give me a chance to get out of the hot sun and get me closer to all this activity over here.

"OK."

I agree to it, but I go back across the street to talk to Victor about it. I tell him the deal, and he thinks it's a good deal. If he thinks I should do it, then I'm going to do it. I trust him.

"I'm not sure about this donation thing."

"Well, I'm sure you are going to make out just fine over there."

A few days later, I set up shop at the Downtown Club. I have nice shade, but no one is stopping for shoeshines. At first, I'm thinking this is a complete bust.

"You're over here now, huh?"

It's Clovis City Councilmember Bob Whalen.

My first customer at the Downtown Club is Bob Whalen. Bless his heart. Good old Bob. When Victor comes out of the club after lunch, he tells his friends that Karl's a good shoeshine and that they should get their shoes shined.

Others start following Bob Whalen's lead. And I make a lot of friends. I'm making about the same as I did across the street, but this is a different atmosphere. I have more credibility working out of the Downtown Club.

I leave every day at three in the afternoon when the club closes and then head over to the Mediterranean place to take out the trash to earn an additional ten bucks a day. Now I'm making like fifty dollars on a good day.

I'm starting to get to know the members of the club. I'm not that busy shining shoes, but I jump up and open the door for them. I welcome them. It's not my job, but I like doing it. I don't like not being busy.

The valet guy, Mike, is real busy. He's on his own because the other valet guy got sick. Today is a particularly busy day at the club and there are like ten cars backed up to be parked.

"Dude, let me help you out."

"I can't. I will get in trouble if I let you park the cars."

"What do you mean? I have a driver's license."

I do. That's one of the first things I did when I got out. I knew I would need it for a job.

"Sorry, man. I can't let you help."

This is driving me nuts, just sweeping the sidewalk and watching him be all busy. After the lunch rush, I go to talk to Vanessa. She agrees to let me work as a valet, since they are one man down on the valet parking.

"But I want you tending the door. I'm getting a lot of compliments about you at the door."

This feels great. I'm just so relieved to be busy. The next day, I get there an hour early just to prepare. Now, I'm actually on payroll. I'm going to actually earn a paycheck instead of donations for shining shoes.

The first car I park is a beautiful red Lexus with leather seats. All the cars are brand-new cars. Just beautiful cars. I'm really careful, making sure I go slow and park the cars just right. It's hopping, and I love this pace.

The big bummer is that with this new position, I'm also in charge of cleaning the bathrooms. I'm not thrilled about that part of the job, but I will take the bad with the good. I am an employee of the Downtown Club. This means something.

Only takes a few days to get the kinks out. Mike and I are like a well-oiled machine.

One day I've just gotten through cleaning the bathrooms and preparing for the lunch rush when a newspaper in the lobby catches my eye.

Headline says something about the homeless camp to be demolished.

I pick up the newspaper and read the story. This means that my homeless camp will be demolished. That night, I tell Big Nate about it. He says that the City of Fresno people have been coming around, telling us that we need to clear all of our stuff or they will take it.

Several weeks later, a guy from the City of Fresno comes by and invites some of us to apply for the Fresno First Steps Home program. I don't know anything about this. I'm thinking the program may be a good thing, though, since I've been wanting to get out of here.

I go to this building down the street and stand in line. The lady I get to is really nice and asks me all kinds of questions. She hands me a form and asks if I can read and write.

Of course I can read and write! Do you think I'm some kind of dummy?

I fill it out and hand it back in. I'm supposed to wait, and then I'm called back up.

"You qualify, Mr. Johnson."

"OK. For what?"

"Well, we are going to put you in a motel first until your background check comes back."

Unbelievable.

I get back to the camp, and there's a bunch of chaos. Big Nate is talking to a guy with a microphone, and a TV camera is on him. I can't hear exactly what he's saying, but he's saying something like they can't take our stuff and make us move.

I understand how he feels. This is his home. He's been here for eight years. But I kind of agree with what the city is doing—saying that everyone deserves to have a safe place to live and to live with dignity and trying to find real homes for the people in the camp. This may have been Big Nate's home for the past eight years, but it is not safe and it is not comfortable.

This group of people who call themselves Occupy Fresno show up and try to organize us to protest. I don't plan on protesting anything. I plan to cooperate with the people who are trying to help me. I don't understand why people are so upset at the mayor for trying to help us get housing. It is a little upsetting to see your tent taken down, though.

There is a lot of drama going on. Lots of resistance. The city is coming in to tear down the camp. It's not like we haven't been given the notice. They have been here talking with people, letting them know where they can go.

I lived in that homeless camp for eight months. Now I'm getting put up in a motel. I'm a little scared because I'm not sure what I'm supposed to be doing to look for a place. Other than Kern Street and Courthouse Park—well, and the Greyhound Bus Station—I don't know this town.

The people from the Fresno Housing Authority are just so nice. Tiffany Cantu is one of the best people I meet. She reminds me of Mama, taking care of people. She comes in her truck and gets my stuff and takes me to the motel where I will stay until my background check comes back. If all checks out as I told them, I can then find an apartment. She's telling me about the program and all the rules. There's lots of paperwork that she's filling out for me. I can tell she really cares about her job—just like Mama cared about her job.

The City of Fresno gives us claim forms to file regarding any of our personal belongings that got destroyed during the clean-up. I fill mine out and hand it over. Then, all these lawyers start showing up, talking to all of us about how it wasn't right for the city to destroy the place where we lived and take all of our things. They take all my information and say that I'm part of a lawsuit. I'm not paying too much attention to all of that because I feel like I'm being taken care of.

I just need to find an apartment, and I'm not sure where to start. I don't really know this town—all I know is that I have to be close to my job because I love it at the Downtown Club. I reach out to Victor to explain what's going on. He's my advisor, and I know he will know what to do. Victor takes me out one day during lunchtime to look at apartments and pick up applications.

After I've been in the motel for several weeks, Tiffany comes by to check in with me.

"Karl, you have to find a place. You are only here in the motel for another two weeks."

"I don't know the streets. I just don't know where to go."

Tiffany tells me to get into her truck. She drives me to an apartment complex not far from downtown. I'm not thrilled with what I see. It's not that the apartment is bad—it's just that the people around here are no good. I can just tell by the young men walking down the street that things are a little rough here. Tiffany says I need to start somewhere, and I can change later. I just need to get into a place.

So, now I have an apartment. I can't wait to tell Victor. Even though the apartment complex wasn't my first choice, I'm excited. And I can tell Victor is pleased. He arranges for a housewarming party at his office. I'm so amazed by all the gifts I get from his coworkers—they all know me. They are so generous. I get a coffee pot, dishes, cleaning supplies—I am well set for my first place of my own since getting out of prison. A couple of my lawyer clients bring me some furniture—a table, a couch, and even a TV.

Now I'm really excited about moving into my new apartment. In late November, just after Thanksgiving, I move into my apartment with the help of Tiffany and her white truck. We get all the stuff into the apartment, and when I close the door behind her, I look around. There's a little living room, a small kitchen on the other side of the wall with a place for a little kitchen table, and a bathroom with a single sink, toilet, and shower. And one bedroom—just for me.

Wow. This is mine.

First thing I do is go take a long, hot shower. The worst part of being homeless is not being able to clean yourself up when you want to. I don't have to go stand in line at the Poverello House to shower anymore. I can take a shower whenever I want to. This is my own shower, and I stay in there for almost an hour.

I go make sure that I locked the front door. That's another thing that you don't get to do when you are homeless—there are no locks on your tent and no control over your own safety.

I don't have a bed yet, but that's all right with me. I lie down in the bedroom on the floor. I have some blankets and a pillow, so I'm in good shape. I'm looking up at the ceiling, trying to remember all the bedroom ceilings I have stared up at—my most favorite being the bedroom I shared with Lil' Red, Gary, and David when we lived in Wilmington. Talking about making it big in the NBA and how we would take care of each other.

What happened to those dreams?

I realize in this moment that I expected Lil' Red to take care of me because that was our pact—whoever makes it big has to take care of the others. What a fool I have been.

I have to take care of myself.

I used to ride along with the arrogance of having a brother who was an NBA All-Star—just going through life thinking that the world owed me.

The world owes me nothing. But I owe it to Lil' Red and Mama to lift myself.

By the time the lawyers get around to interviewing me about my damages, I'm in my apartment, thanks to Fresno First Steps Home. I take one look at the paper that says the lawsuit is against the City of Fresno and Mayor Ashley Swearengin and tell the lawyer I don't want to be a part of the lawsuit anymore.

I can't sue the city that helped me. The city doesn't owe me—I owe the city for getting me off the streets.

I didn't get into my new apartment until after Thanksgiving, so I'm excited to have a place to be for Christmas. I get a string of lights and a small Christmas tree at the Dollar Store. I even buy a little wreath to put on my front door. The Christmas lights in my front window send a message of season's greetings to my neighbors.

I want the world to see my joy.

Chapter Twenty-Two

The ache for home lives in all of us, the safe place where we can go as we are and not be questioned.
—Maya Angelou

I am so grateful to the City of Fresno and to the mayor, who is putting a lot of political capital on the line to address homelessness. Fresno First Steps Home has saved my life. All I needed was a place to live so that I could get all the other pieces of my life together. That's the case for so many people who find themselves homeless.

There are several others living in my apartment complex who have benefitted from Fresno First Steps Home. People like Betty, who lives upstairs. She's a really nice self-proclaimed "farm girl" from Iowa who just got caught up with the wrong people and the wrong stuff. Same thing with Randy, who found himself living on the streets after his wife kicked him out for using drugs. It's such a mistake to get caught up in the wrong drug-using crowd, but just like me, they have a second chance.

People are always moving in and moving out of my apartment complex. There's a big black wrought-iron fence off the parking lot that closes off the courtyard. It's clean, but there's a lot of activity here—most of it not good. I keep to myself for the most part to steer clear of any bad business.

Even though there is not a lot of stability, I do have a sense of community here. I always find a community wherever I am—but that's just me. In the homeless camp, we had a community, and in prison, I had a community. I suppose it's human nature to want to belong. I just want to be a part of a good community. I want to contribute and be a part of something good.

Betty upstairs cooks for me a lot. She makes real dinners—tells me about the big meat packs from the store. She gives me the hot dogs because she doesn't eat hot dogs.

"Hey Karl, I'm making chicken tonight. Wanna come up?"

I'm tired, and the thought of trying to figure out what to eat for dinner makes me even more tired. I take her up on the offer. Betty is a really nice lady. She's been through a lot—just like so many who find themselves homeless.

"Sure. I'll be up in a bit."

On top of her TV, there's a picture of her at her high school graduation—something that she's proud of and she should be. People make lots of assumptions about the homeless—that they're uneducated, crazy, drug addicts. It's a generalization that doesn't begin to capture reality. Betty tells me that she just got caught up with the wrong group of people.

Sounds familiar.

The difference is that she was a follower of the bad stuff, and I was a leader of the bad stuff. I was one of those wrong people she hung out with. She shares things about her family—the sadness in her eyes I recognize as regret.

Her apartment is just like mine, but a little cleaner, I have to admit. She has a lot of little trinkets, and completed jigsaw puzzles hang on her walls for art. There's another puzzle in the works on the little coffee table—it's a scene of Central Park in the fall. I have never been to New York City, and I wonder if DJ ever got a chance to visit Central Park when he was in town to play the Knicks.

"I like this one that you got going."

"It keeps my mind off things," she says.

I know what she's talking about. The regret and guilt are enough to kill you. It's the draw of the drugs—to mute the pain. Sometimes the pain of regret is enough to choke me—I just can't breathe. It's a vicious cycle—do drugs, feel the pain of regret, do drugs again to get rid of the pain.

Pain—I have to face the pain. Learning that life is not all fun and games is a hard pill to swallow. But the ups and the downs are what help you live in the middle.

The next day, I'm in the courtyard, and I look up to see a black guy knocking on Betty's door. I haven't seen him before, so I'm immediately suspicious. There have been a few boyfriends here and there—and not the good kind. That's the problem with being a follower—you just blindly trust and follow others, rarely standing up for yourself. This makes Betty gullible.

Betty is like my sister, and I don't want her to get hurt, so I head upstairs. I knock on her door.

"I got some company," she says as she opens the door.

"That's all right. I got something to talk to you about."

I walk into her apartment, and the guy is just looking at me.

"Can you come back later?"

"Nah, I can't come back. Just give me a minute."

I'm eyeing this guy, as he's leaning against the wall looking right back at me. He's standing right next to this big old flat-screen TV.

Something's not right. This guy doesn't look right.

"I'm taking care of some business. Can I talk to you later?" Betty says, as she tries to move me to the door.

This is the second time she says this, so I know I need to go out of respect for her.

The next morning I go and check on Betty to make sure she's all right.

"I'm here to check out the TV," I say.

She lets me in and sits on the couch.

"Well, it doesn't work. I gave that guy a hundred bucks and the thing doesn't work."

"What? Didn't you check it before you handed him the cash?"

She just looks at me with sadness in her eyes. Now I'm mad. I'm pissed at that guy for beating a hundred bucks out of her, and I'm pissed at her for being so gullible. I tell the property manager about it—he got a good look at the guy, so I tell him if he sees that guy again, let me know. He owes Betty a hundred bucks.

I tell everyone about this. The thing is that she's like a sister to me, and we are neighbors. She didn't do anything to this guy for him to beat that money out of her. We got to take care of each other. It's just not right what happened to her. I'm telling my neighbor who lives on the other side of me about what happened. I listen to myself tell the story, and it hits me: *how is this any different than all the dealings I did in my previous life?*

The difference is that now I have a conscience—I didn't have one before because of all the drugs. It just isn't right, and I'm not going to stand for it.

I'm at work a couple of weeks later when the guy comes back to take the TV and give Betty her money back. I'm not sure how it happened—it just did. The property manager and I make a pact with Betty that she needs to come to us if someone wants to sell her something.

All is right with the world again.

I get a call from someone at the Fresno Housing Authority, asking me if I can go to a special fundraising event for Fresno First Steps Home. She tells me that I should be prepared to tell my story about my transformation from homelessness to living a regular life.

Once she tells me the mayor is going to be there, I'm in. And I do feel a sense of obligation to Fresno First Steps Home—the program saved my life by giving me a real place to live. There's something about the mayor that I am so impressed with—I have watched her come and go at the Downtown Club, and she's always put together. She's a very nice-looking young lady—ice-blue eyes and blond hair. But more than that, she's smart. I see her on TV and listen to her on the radio, and I'm telling you, she is smart and savvy. She gets it, and I know she leads from the right place—from the heart. I hear her talk about homelessness and how everyone deserves to have a safe place to live. You would think everyone feels that way, but they don't. Homelessness—like so many issues—is a hot political topic because you have the "rights" of the homeless and their property, and you have the public health issue.

I get to bring two guests with me, so that's an easy decision for me—Victor and my boss, Vanessa. The event will be held in the evening at a restaurant downtown. I'm so excited and nervous, so I write down some of my thoughts on a piece of paper. Vanessa and I walk over to the restaurant together, and we meet Victor there.

When we walk into the restaurant, there are so many people. We have to check in and make sure our names are on the list. It's an extra security measure because US Secretary for Housing and Urban Development Shaun Donovan is there.

They did not tell me that.

Now I'm really excited because I love politics and this guy is on President Obama's cabinet. I can't tell if I'm more excited or nervous. The two of these emotions are exploding in my chest.

"I need a drink," I say to Victor.

I really need to calm my nerves.

"Probably best to wait until after you speak to have that drink," Victor advises.

He's doing a good job keeping me calm. I see a lot of familiar faces from the Downtown Club—city council members and business leaders. I hear a lot of, "Hey, Karl!" My head is spinning a bit, and I feel like I may not be able to speak in front of all these important people. I take a deep breath and take it all in—I actually feel really important. It's like I have something to contribute.

"Hi, Karl. Would you mind going upstairs to do a couple of TV interviews with the mayor?" a friendly young woman asks. I nod and follow her up the stairs.

I get to the top of the stairs and see all the bright lights, cameras, and white screens. And there across the room is the mayor all lit up in the glow of the lights. She's wearing her signature red. Poised and in control like she is all the time, she's talking to a reporter.

I want to ask her, "How can you be smart and pretty at the same time and have good sense?"

As if all these people didn't make me nervous enough, seeing all these TV cameras is so overwhelming. I stand there for a bit, and the mayor gets up from her seat to greet me.

"Hi, Karl. It's good to see you—how are you doing?" The mayor is so sincere.

"Hi, Mayor. I'm doing great."

"Thank you for being here. We are thrilled you are willing to share your story."

"We need to get the program started." The friendly young woman comes back and directs her comments to the mayor.

We go back downstairs, and I notice something about the room—it's bustling with energy and laughter. People are having a good time, drinking wine and cocktails. It hits me in that moment that I'm in control—that's the secret of public speaking. Get everyone loose with a few drinks; then it's easier to tell a few jokes. Victor told me to start out with a joke. I'm not really the joke-telling type, but I'm listening to his every advice because this is all new for me.

The mayor introduces me to Secretary Donovan. I shake his hand and stand right next to him, as the mayor goes to the microphone. I'm having a hard time keeping myself together. I can't really hear what she is saying because my heart is pounding in my ears. I think about DJ and wonder if his heart pounded in his ears right before a championship game.

"I'm pleased to introduce Karl Johnson."

Man, I'm not ready for this.

I shake her hand with the notes clutched in my other hand, then walk toward the microphone.

"Thank you. You know what, I wrote some notes for this, but I'm just gonna wing it."

The room laughs—there is warmth and acceptance coming from that crowd's laughter. Now I know what Victor meant when he told me that everyone in the room wants me to do good. This laughter tells me that this is going to be all right.

"I know a lot of you guys from the Downtown Club, and I bet you didn't know that I was homeless. I came downtown every day, and I was cleaned up. I took a shower every day and came here to work to be respectable. But I did all of that living out of a tent."

There are not any gasps in the room, but the expressions on some of their faces tell me that this was a surprise to them. I go on to tell the highlights of my story. I'm hoping that my words underscore the fact that you shouldn't judge people if you don't know their circumstances.

"You know what? There's someone more important in the room tonight than me that needs to speak, so I'm going to pass the microphone to United States HUD Secretary Shaun Donovan."

I feel like my body goes limp with relief as I pass the microphone to Secretary Donovan. I make a beeline to the bar. That's my reward for getting up in front of all these important people to share my story.

Then I hear: "Hey, where is Karl Johnson at?"

It's Secretary Donovan, and he's speaking right to me in front of all these people. I'm almost to the bar when he says:

"Let's get Karl Johnson back up here."

Damn. I thought I was done.

If a US secretary tells you to do something, you do it. So, I head back up there, and he says, "I just want you to know that there's no one more important in this room than you."

Wow. That blows me away.

I manage a "thank you" and head back to the bar.

Victor and I go after the shrimp. I'm having such a great time. This is incredible. The energy in the room is like nothing I have felt before—it's so positive. I'm used to groups of people, but not groups of people all focused on doing a great thing. I feel like I'm a part of something important.

A woman from PG&E gets up to talk. I'm still calming myself down from all that excitement when I hear her announce a $35,000 donation to Fresno First Steps Home.

Wow.

Then she says something that catches my attention.

"The ache for home lives in all of us, the safe place where we can go as we are and not be questioned."

She is quoting Maya Angelou. These words go straight to my heart. It's as if I am the only one in the room. They are simple words, but their meaning is so deep and revealing. Home is a safe place. That's what Mama's house was to me—safe. And she didn't question me. I was accepted for me. That's what home is.

Every day can't be a party. It's taken me almost a lifetime to learn this. Every drug addict needs to learn this. Drugs take away your ability to cope with the ups and downs of life. Going through life high all the time didn't give me the tools to deal with everyday life.

And it's not just the ups and downs of life. It's the pain and the regret that can kill you. How easy it would be to turn my back on the pain and the regret I feel every day and reach for the cocaine. Numb the pain and wash away the regret. The GUILT.

That night after the event, I pull out my journal. The excitement of the night has led to a strange sadness and I need to write about it. I have so many thoughts swimming through my head. Writing gives me a chance to have a conversation with myself. That's the thing about me—I can have a conversation with myself because I have so much to say.

> *To me it's simply about living this day as if it were your last day. I truly need to keep my head on straight and my mind focused on moving forward. I have had enough downs. It's time to have more ups. I'm lonely here without my family, and I miss my brother Dennis so much it hurts. Well, Karl, you are a grown-ass man. I climbed hills in fire camp with that 40-pound backpack on my back, paying my best for the violations I committed and laws that I broke in my addiction. That's a long time ago when I did not care, so as I will say at the end, I truly miss my brother and my best friend, DJ, because now I have to analyze games by myself. We had so many times when we talked basketball, and I never got tired. He did, though, and he let me know, but I knew I was holding on to my friend, a brother. When you are there surviving the struggle, it's amazing at the end to see what hard work does for a person. I see all the rejection he had to face, and my brother never wavered—he was steadfast taking care of his family, always in the business of staying employed and moving forward. I mean, depending on which way your life goes; for me it was series of bad choices that I made that sent me in a tailspin for a while. But I am back in the game and need to keep headed in the right direction because I need to keep doing the right thing in my life. I need to start thinking about the rest of my life.*

Chapter Twenty-Three

Push yourself again and again. Don't give an inch until the final buzzer sounds.
—Larry Bird

I'm so happy to have my own place and my own shower. I can't help but feel guilty, though. I'm thinking about all my former neighbors in the homeless camp, wondering where they are on this cold, foggy January day.

I'm cleaning up at the club after lunch and taking the leftover food out to the alley to throw it away. This just kills me. I've asked several times if I can take it and give it to others who are hungry. I'm told that because of liability reasons we can't give out the food. My heart is heavy as I dump several pounds of cooked meat and a bunch of rolls into the Dumpster. This waste of good food makes me feel really bad.

Not only does Fresno get really hot in the summer, but it also gets really cold in the winter. The wet fog just bites through your skin, making your bones cold. There's a dude in a sleeping bag huddled up against the building many mornings when I arrive at work. Part of my job is to make sure the building is clear of any homeless people when the members come for lunch.

"Hey man, you can't stay here."

He looks up with a blank stare.

"Yeah, you gotta move on down the road. You hungry?"

He nods his head. I just hate this. I don't want him feeling bad about himself.

"OK, I'll tell you what. You need to go to the Poverello House. They will take care of you there. Just go on down the road and get yourself some food there."

He still doesn't say anything, but he does get up, which means he understands what I'm saying. He climbs out of his sleeping bag and rolls it up. He's really dirty. I just wish he would take care of himself. No one's gonna care about you unless you care about yourself.

I turn, taking a deep breath, and walk back into the warm club.

Why is this so hard?

The heaviness in my heart comes with a nametag: GUILT.

I have a job. I have a place to live and food to eat. But I also have a lot of responsibilities now. I have to pay my bills and make sure I get to work on time every day. There's the rent, which really is not that much thanks to Fresno First Steps Home program, and then there's the utilities to keep my place warm and my lights on. With whatever is left, I buy food and things like toilet paper and dish soap. I suppose this is what normal living is. Now my guilt turns into envy for that guy in the sleeping bag—he doesn't have any bills hanging over his head. No one depends on him for anything.

I get busy with cleaning the bathrooms to get my mind off all this crazy thinking.

"Hey, Karl. They are calling us in for a special meeting," Mike says, as he comes into the bathroom.

"What's going on?"

"I don't know, man. We all need to go into the dining room for a meeting."

This doesn't sound good to me. I know that the club has been having some financial problems. They even brought in a well-known restaurant guy to try to change things up a bit to get the club moving in a more positive direction.

The new manager of the Downtown Club calls an emergency meeting of all employees. "Due to financial challenges, the Downtown Club is closing," he says. "Today is your last day."

That's it. I don't have a job now. It's the only thing that kept me going. Parking cars and shining shoes.

I'm a little panicked.

What do I do now?

I have to find another place to shine shoes.

I go back to the card room and ask to talk to the manager, but he's busy. Then I remember a guy I met at the Downtown Club who owns another building adjacent to the courthouse. It's called the Patterson Building. I head over there and ask to meet with him. The secretary tells me that he's not in, so I leave my name and tell her I'll be back.

Things were going so well. I was on the right track with an actual paycheck and money to pay my own bills. I head home and try to keep my mind from racing. I recognize this feeling. It's the strong survival instinct that I have.

Don't panic. Don't get crazy. It will all work out.

It's all I can do to keep my mind from racing. I know that I will find a way to keep my place, but I just don't trust myself. The lure of the dark side strengthens when things get tough. It's a way to mute the worry and the heartsickness. I lie in my bed, willing myself to stay positive. I owe it to Mama and Dennis to stay on this path.

The next day, I go back to the Patterson Building. One of the owners, Jeff Roush, is in, and the secretary is really nice to me, as if she was waiting for me. Jeff's a nice guy and says the building has a small shoeshine place on the alley-side of the building that has not been in operation for several years. I tell him that I have a solid following. We strike a deal—I do a little work keeping the outside of the building looking nice, I get to run my business in the small space.

He walks me down there and unlocks the door. It's a heavy steel door and we struggle to get it open. Once we pull back the door, I can't believe what I'm seeing. It's the coolest little space.

There's a built-in, carpeted perch for my customers to sit on with two metal footrests for them to prop their feet on. The walls are covered in business cards, and there is a mounted box that says "Holy Bible." There's a phone, a fan, a TV, and a small refrigerator.

I can't believe how lucky I am.

"I don't want any problems. You do a good job and you have this space," Jeff says.

Once he leaves, I inspect my new space. It needs a good cleaning. The calendar on the wall still reads May 2009—nearly four years ago. Must be the last time someone was here. That someone was Lester Jackson, as the yellowed *Fresno Bee* article tacked to the wall indicates. It's a two-page spread written about Lester and his shoe-shining business in this very space.

I read the article and get chills. This is so cool. I go over to the metal cabinet and open it up. I can't believe my eyes. There are about forty brand-new shoe polishes in there! They are the Kiwi brand—the best. I have struck gold.

I open my shoeshine place and call it Anytime Shoe Shine. At first, I don't have very many customers, but I'm not going to give up. Money is tight, and I'm trying to make all this work without an actual paycheck.

Temptations are everywhere, every day. It's a daily battle, but it's a battle worth fighting. Life is challenging, but it's how you respond to the challenges. I heard once that life is 10 percent what happens to you and 90 percent how you react to it. I'm in control of that 90 percent, and I'm going to make sure that 90 percent is filled with the right stuff.

I go down to the Poverello House once a week to buy shoes. I buy them for a couple bucks and fix them up, so I can give shoes to people who don't have anything on their feet.

There's this guy who is always walking by, and he doesn't have any shoes. It's just driving me crazy, seeing him walking down the street with no shoes. I find a pair of sneakers at the Poverello House that I think will fit him. I take them back to my shoeshine place and clean them up real good. I put them aside for him until he comes walking by. Sure enough, here he comes.

"Hey, man! I got some shoes for you!"

He looks up and can barely see through that mop of curly hair on his head.

"Don't need no shoes," I hear him mumble.

"Everybody's got to have some shoes. You come over here now. You can't be walking around with no shoes on—it's just no good for your feet."

I tell him to sit down on the little stool just outside my shoeshine room. I don't hand the shoes over to him because I can't trust him to put them on himself.

He's still mumbling to himself about not needing any shoes. I don't pay him any mind as I tell him to put his feet in the damn shoes.

"Now, look there. Those shoes looking good," I say as I back away, making sure he doesn't kick his foot up right into my face.

He stands, looking down at his new shoes. He looks up at me. I can see his eyes for a brief moment through that curly mop, and while there is no smile on his face, there is gratitude in his eyes.

"You keep those shoes on your feet as you walk around down here."

He's like a child who doesn't like to be told what to do. I know this feeling all too well. But damn it—you gotta wear shoes if you're walking around downtown.

He turns and shuffles away, as I think about Mama. Thoughts of Mama running around the neighborhood, dropping off food and clothing for families that needed help fill my head. Daddy didn't like Mama being out so late—he even got a little suspicious that she was out messing around. But I knew better. Mama was out there in the projects, helping families.

"I know my kids are eating every night, but what about those other kids who are going without food?"

She would explain what she was doing to Daddy, trying to get him to understand. Mama was passionate about taking care of people. And that's my passion now too. I'm just so thankful to have this opportunity to finally give back—to take care of people.

I'm trying to get away from using street words when I talk to professional people, but you can only be who you are. I want to be a professional person, but inside, the street person is still inside me.

Shoe shining is tough business, though. Guys come by and say they will be back in an hour with their shoes, and they don't show up. I am struggling financially, but trying not to panic. I need to trust this path I am on.

There's this girl who lives in the park in front of the courthouse. No one likes her. She's not the best-looking girl. I can't stand in judgment of whatever she's on, but I can help her with her shoes.

She's another one with no shoes. Her name is Sally. I'm a little irritated with her. Actually, I'm pissed off at her because I just gave her a pair of boots and she's not wearing them. I gave her a pair of shoes once, and then when I saw her the next week, she was barefoot again. But I realize that she has a hard time with tying shoes—or anything with a zipper.

In the back of my shop, I have these women's shoes with an elastic strap. I'm fixing them for her. When I see her, I'm going to give her these shoes that I fixed up.

All I can do is to make her feet better by giving her some good shoes.

Shoe shining is not just about smoothing out the scuffs and polishing the shine back in shoes. It's about the conversation. I just like to talk to people. People are interesting to me. I am never short on words, either. I can talk about anything.

I'm shining this lawyer guy's shoes, and he's asking me how my business is going.

"You know. There's good days and bad days, but people gotta get their shoes shined."

"Are you from Fresno?"

"No, man. I'm from Compton."

"How did you end up here?"

Man, it's a long story.

"Well, why don't you give me the highlights?"

The whole damn story is a highlight.

I tell him about growing up in Compton, and about being one of sixteen kids. I tell him that I have been working since I was thirteen and how I got caught up in some bad stuff.

He's asking me lots of questions, but it doesn't make me nervous. I like this guy.

Then I get to the part about my Mama dying and about my hero dying. How the two most important people in my life died while I was in prison. I have heard myself tell my story many times. But today it feels different. Today, these words are heavy with emotion.

"Your brother was DJ?"

"Yeah, man, and he was such a good person."

He's hung up on the fact that DJ's brother is in Fresno, shining shoes. I get this a lot. So, I pull out the wedding photo of Dennis and Donna with both families in the photo. I carry this photo in my backpack. Sort of like proof that I'm not some kind of nut case, making crazy claims.

There's Dennis and Donna in the middle. Mama is holding onto Dennis's arm sort of protective-like. She has on a simple floral dress with a corsage. I'm kneeling down, and I'm not smiling. None of my brothers and sisters is smiling in this photo. On Donna's side, her sister, her mama, and her aunt are all lined up in beautiful gowns with big old smiles on their faces. Her daddy is standing behind her mama—you can't even see his face.

For years, I looked at this photo and felt the loss. I always thought his wedding day was the day we lost Dennis. I figured we were just the poor family from the projects, and Donna's side was like the royal family with their prince who was getting ready to rule the world.

I finish shining the lawyer's shoes. He climbs down from the perch, and he's smiling at his shoes.

"Now that's a shine to make you smile!" I say.

"Thanks. Good luck, Karl."

I watch him walk away and realize that the bitterness I have felt for Donna all these years doesn't live within me anymore. I was so focused on my loss of Dennis.

How he wasn't coming around to visit. How he wasn't giving me the money or the stuff I wanted. She was just protecting her husband.

When he died, I felt true loss.

And now, I feel sadness for Donna—for her losing her husband, her life partner.

When Dennis died, I lost my identity. I held onto the hope of "crossing that bridge" with him when I got out of prison, but it didn't happen. My path was more than undefined—it didn't exist.

I realize in this moment that the path I am meant to travel is up to me—no one else. Dennis didn't owe me anything because of his fame and his perceived fortune. I owe him a life filled with hard work and determination—that was his legacy—and that's what I intend to fulfill.

Although I'm determined to work hard, money is just really tight for a while. I'm not making enough to survive.

But, like a gift from God, the news of the Downtown Club reopening hits. I can't believe it. A guy named Nick Farid bought the restaurant and is reopening it.

I have to meet this guy.

I go over to the Downtown Club and ask for him. I explain that I used to work there, parking cars and shining shoes. He's a good guy and says that he wants to rehire all the old staff. I can't believe my luck.

Downtown Fresno is on the rebound. This is a good sign. It feels right, and the excitement to be back there working is only amplified by a story in the *Fresno Bee* that says:

"And Karl Johnson and his big smile are back as valet and doorman (though his shoeshine business has moved to the Patterson building on Fulton Mall)."

This makes me feel so good. That small mention gave a big boost to my shoeshine operation, too.

This town is filled with good people like Victor Salazar who have shown an interest in me. They have extended good will. It's my turn to contribute to this good will.

My opportunity to formally be a part of this good will comes in the form of an invitation to serve on the Fresno County Local Board for the Emergency Food and Shelter Program. I get a call from a woman at the United Way. They have been looking for someone like me to serve on the board.

I'm a little nervous because I have never been a board member before, but I go to the first meeting, and everyone is so nice. I'm sitting at the table with the people who run the organizations who have helped me.

I don't feel like I can contribute a whole lot to the discussion, so I just listen. I have a lot of learning to do. But I do know how it is to be homeless and in need of emergency food and shelter. I am amazed by how much is being done in this town to help others, but overwhelmed because I know that there are so many people who need this help.

I walk out of that first meeting with a little spring in my step. I realize that I have purpose—I can contribute in a formal way to helping others.

Purpose. I have a purpose.

Everyone needs a purpose, and I have mine.

Chapter Twenty-Four

In the Final Moments

The best player I ever played with was Dennis Johnson.
—Larry Bird

I miss DJ so much. Watching basketball is just not the same. Now I have to analyze the games all by myself. We had so many times when we talked basketball together, and I never got tired of it. Dennis has given me the will to survive and the realization that hard work does pay off. I see all the rejection my brother had to face, but he never wavered—he was steadfast in taking care of his family and always in the business of staying employed and moving forward.

That was the difference between us—he was focused on the long term, and I was focused on the short term. I just want to yell out from the top of the mountain to know-it-all kids how important their decisions are and how they can affect you for the rest of your life. The guilt, regret, and loneliness are the debt I pay for all my bad decisions, but I'm back in the game with the promise of living a life I'm meant to live.

I miss the comfort of Mama's home. She just made everything right, and she never judged me. It's time for me to make things right for myself. She showed me the way.

I pull out Mama's letters from the drawer by my bed. It's hard for me to read her words. It still hurts so much. I am now able to feel what she might have been feeling, having to write her son in prison. The guilt of that cuts through me—I just wanted her to be proud of me. I unfold one of her last letters:

> *Karl, we all miss you and are praying for you to be out soon. I hope you can read my writing. It is hard with one eye to write sometime, but you know what? I am not going to complain because I have had a good life and I am so thankful that God let me live to see all my children grow up. Well, Karl, I will be writing soon. We all love you and miss you, so don't feel bad if some of us don't write because it is hard for some of your brothers and sisters to do this.*
>
> *Your mom,*
> *Margaret Johnson*

Now that I know how to use a computer, I can find my way around the Internet pretty good. Tim Cox, my shoeshine client and now my really good friend, lets me use a computer in his law office. Tim is such a good person. He's an attorney who helps the homeless and those who don't have a lot of money. He's been so good to me, teaching me how to use the computer. I didn't even know what a mouse was, let alone how to use it, and he taught me.

I know what I want to find on the Internet. I want to see Gary's speech at the Hall of Fame induction again.

I was still in fire camp when DJ was inducted into the Naismith Memorial Basketball Hall of Fame. I couldn't watch the ceremony on TV, but Hot Link and I would talk about it while working in the laundry.

"Don't cry, man—just be happy," Hot Link had said.

My heart ached for Dennis. After all that he went through and all the hard work, he couldn't be there for this, his own induction. This honor was the ultimate achievement—he did it. He not only made it in the NBA—he achieved the top of his game.

A quick search gets me to the Naismith Memorial Basketball Hall of Fame website. I click on the "Hall of Famers" button, and I look through the names in alphabetical order. Dennis Johnson.

Click.

There he is. The website reads:

> *"In the final moments and closing seconds of the games that mattered most, Dennis Johnson always rose to the occasion. During his 14-year NBA career, the defensive-minded point guard played for the Seattle SuperSonics, the Phoenix Suns, and the Boston Celtics...His quick hands and sure feet made him a constant threat to steal the ball and lead the fast break, creating instant offense for his teammates...In Game 5 of the 1987 Eastern Conference Finals, he cemented his Celtic legacy when he displayed his uncanny court sense and cut to the basket, taking the pass from Larry Bird and putting up a twisting layup at the buzzer to defeat the Pistons."*

I scroll down the page and see a picture of Gary with an arrow in the middle of it. I click the arrow, and a video starts.

"Representing Dennis Johnson are his widow, Donna, and his brother, Gary Johnson, who are welcomed by Larry Bird," the announcer says.

There's Gary with Donna sitting right behind. They get up to go to the stage, walking down the red-carpeted aisle. I see Gary reach down for Donna's hand.

I see Larry Bird join them on stage, and Gary reaches for a piece of paper in this jacket pocket as he takes the podium.

There is my brother, Gary, standing on that Basketball Hall of Fame stage. I'm so proud of him.

"Thank you. Humbling. It is so humbling. I'm just here to say 'thanks' for my brother. He was such a great guy."

I can tell he's nervous.

"I know that he would want me to thank everyone who got him here. But first of all, we would have to mention God."

He clears his throat.

"I want to say thanks to Donna."

The camera moves to her.

Gary continues to thank everyone, including Larry Bird. His voice breaks a little, and I think he's going to cry.

"DJ would want to thank our Mom and Dad. They taught him everything. My Dad was a good Dad. My Mom just didn't have any quit in her."

"It was obvious…being the guy he is, Dennis never knew when to quit. He just never gave up."

"Thanks to my brother, Charles, who was his main influence and our family's inspiration."

Gary goes on to talk about Charlie.

"He taught two brothers how to swim, and he didn't even know how to swim."

Gary talks about Kenny. How Kenny worked with Dennis's jump shot. He thanks Dennis's coaches, particularly Lenny Wilkens. "Thanks for giving my brother a chance to start."

He thanks the NBA family for their support. "I love you guys, and I love you guys for loving my brother."

"But there is one other person that I just really want to thank when I got up here. Because I knew I would be nervous because I'm not really a public speaker... There was always one person that kept my brother's name out there... I'd like to thank Charles Barkley for keeping his name out there."

The audience laughs and applauds. The camera turns to Charles Barkley, smiling in the audience, and he gives a little nod.

"Thank you, for Dennis, my brother."

Gary and Donna hug on stage, and the video fades out.

I wish I could have been there.

More than that, I wish I could have been there when Dennis was alive. He was my hero. I could have done more to support him. He made his dream of playing in the NBA a reality. And just as you would find in the real world, there were always challenges. He worked hard and kept at it. But all I saw was my brother as a famous basketball star, making a lot of money.

What I understand now is that we all soar. Some of us soar to really high heights, and some of us just barely get off the ground. Maintaining the flight is the challenge. It is not the destination that is the reward. It is the journey.

It's time for me to give back. Mama and Dennis were so good to me. They gave their lives so that I could have a better one. I will not waste this life anymore. I will carry the torch to help others like Mama did. I will live DJ's legacy of hard work and perseverance.

I always wanted DJ and Mama to think I was a good guy—that I was worthy of being their son and their brother. When I was at the lowest of the low, I did not believe

I had worth. I know now that I am worthy—and with this worth, I have a responsibility to give back and live the life I was meant to live.

Rebound. This is my rightful journey.